How to Use the Internet

Seven Essential Internet Tools and Skills Anyone Can Learn to Use

Juancho Forlanda

ISBN-13: 978-1500293758

Table of Contents

Preface

It's an exciting time we live in today, especially if you live in a country where there is relatively free flow of information and there is easy access to technology.

If you have been meaning to really find out what the fuss is all about regarding the Internet, but have been apprehensive for one reason or another, or maybe you think it is too difficult, now may be the time to change.

The Internet and technology has made the entire world accessible. Life is too short to miss out on what the younger generation and the tech savvy are enjoying right now. Some people who were once technophobic have already made the leap, and are already connected with long lost friends and relatives.

Using technology and accessing the Internet have gotten easier. Open up your mind; tell yourself you can do it, and you will.

I've written this book to help anyone who wishes to learn the use of the Internet, regardless of technical background. This book is designed to help you make the technology leap by identifying seven essential tools and skills that you can easily learn to use.

The book covers three tools and four skills:

- Chapter 1 provides an overview of the seven tools and skills to give the reader a point of reference
- Chapter 2 talks about the first tool--the Internet browser
- Chapter 3 discusses the next tool--email
- Chapter 4 covers the social networking tool
- Chapter 5 talks about the first Internet skill--TEXTing
- Chapter 6 teaches Internet research
- Chapter 7 discusses shopping without bounds
- Chapter 8 talks about online selling--your junk maybe someone else's treasure
- Chapter 9 discusses some final thoughts on using the Internet

Acknowledgement

This book would not have been possible without direct help from my wife, Mercedes, who provided review and editing. Her perspective as a reader helped align the wording and presentation of the information so that the reader can easily grasp the ideas behind the tools and skills presented.

"For the things we have to learn before we can do them, we learn by doing them."

— Aristotle, The Nicomachean Ethics

Introduction

In today's highly gadget-ized society, there is almost no way of going through life without using technology. Technology is everywhere: TV remote control, digital video recorder (DVR), digital cameras, bank ATM, self-serve checkout line at your grocery store, your cell phone, your car's dashboard, and even your gas station's control panel (where you swipe your credit card). Therefore, if you are afraid of technology, it is too late, you've been using them all along without realizing it. Thus, you can easily take that leap towards using gadgets like laptops, tablets, or smart phones. This book is here to help you do that.

This book will show and teach you seven essential technology tools and skills that will aid in your pursuit of success or enjoyment.

The essential tools are:

- Internet Browser - *the window to the Internet*
- Email - *the origin of Internet communication*
- Social Networking - *the platform for connecting/reconnecting with friends & relatives, and discover new ones*

The essential skills are:

- Texting - *the essence of basic digital communication*
- Internet Research - *means to gather information on people, places, and things*
- Online Shopping - *allows you to shop for anything at any time without driving to the store*
- Online Selling - *someone's trash is another's treasure; a means to get rid of things you no longer need*

To those who think they are too old or just not tech savvy enough

The human mind works in mysterious ways but one thing is certain, if you think you can't learn something, your subconscious mind will respond and NOT try to learn.

However, if you tell yourself that you can learn, then your subconscious mind will work to

---

figure out how to understand all the things that may be new to you.

As long as you keep an open mind, you will learn anything you set your mind to. Have faith in yourself.

Internet Browser

Believe it or not, the Internet browser is the window to the Internet. There are several software programs you can use for this, and the choice is really up to you. However, the device you have may dictate which browser you have at the onset. The good news is, you can install the one you like (except on a Chromebook which is limited to using Chrome). The author prefers Google's Chrome as the browser of choice.

These are the built-in Internet browsers for the following devices:

- Windows 7 or 8 computer: Internet Explorer
- Chromebook or Chromebox: Chrome
- Apple iPhone, iTouch, or iPad: Safari
- Android phones or tablets: Android browser

As noted before, if the native browser on your device is not to your liking, you can install your preferred browser as long as your device is not a Chromebook.

You will need an Internet browser in order to support your Internet activities. With today's many options, you can use the Internet browser on any of the following devices or gadgets.

- desktop computer
- laptop computer
- tablet computer
- smartphone

Once you get yourself a device, you are well on your way to taking that first step to learning the essential Internet tools and skills that will help you to pursue success and enjoyment in life.

Email

If you are not familiar with email then think of it as an extremely faster version of the traditional postal mail service. The main difference is, you use your electronic device to send an email correspondence that will reach its destination almost instantly (in a matter of seconds) even when the receiver is halfway around the world.

Email is here to stay even with the advent of new communication mediums (e.g. Facebook, Twitter, Google+). In 2011, a technology market research group (The Radicati Group) estimated that there were 3.1 billion email accounts in use in 2011. They estimate it will rise to 4 billion by 2015 (Email and Webmail Statistics [http://goo.gl/Lpv6BO] by Mark Brownlow, Oct. 2011). Email is still the best non-real time way to communicate with personal or business contacts. It is one of the easiest means to share data with others (e.g. photos, documents). However, it is also one of the biggest source of online junk (i.e. email spam--unsolicited email for some product or service). Nevertheless, knowing how to use email is still crucial to success today.

Social Networking

Think of social networking (e.g. Facebook, Twitter, Google+) as an online bulletin board where people can use an electronic device to share information about what they are doing or what they like. The weird thing is you never really see each other, except for what they post. This is social networking and it is all done through the Internet.

This tool has not been around as long as other means of communication, but it has had one of the biggest impacts on communication within the modern world. Social networking tools include Facebook, Twitter, LinkedIn, and StumbleUpon, just to name a few. The power to share with others has never been so great. It has already shown this power for both personal and professional use. Note that the use of this tool has had its negative impact as well, and knowing how to navigate the social networking world can mean success or failure.

Texting

This is a feature that is often included with your cell phone service. If you have not used texting before, it is possible that you were not made aware of this feature, perhaps you just don't want to deal with it, or maybe you just never found the need for it.

Texting has been around even before cell phones became smart (i.e. the ability to provide access to the Internet and applications). It continues to be the predominant means of real-time communication, especially for the younger generation. 'Real-time', in this context, means that people expect an immediate response to text messages. Since texting uses a different network, it generally works even in places where phone calling services fail.

Texting is crucial for both personal and professional interactions, especially with its seemingly cryptic shorthand or abbreviations. With the advent of smartphones, there are programs/applications (a.k.a. apps) that are available to perform the texting function (e.g.

WhatsApp (http://www.whatsapp.com/) and Text Plus (http://www.textplus.com/)).

Internet Research

Practically everything is on the Internet now.

However, there is a good side and a bad side. The good thing is that you are only a few keystrokes away from information you need. The flip side, all the information out there may require a considerable amount of time to sift through.

Because of this, you will need Internet searching skills to be effective at researching anything.

Online Shopping

The beauty of online shopping is that you are no longer bound by geographical boundaries. Today, with the help of your electronic device, the world is your neighborhood. What you cannot find in your local store, you are bound to find somewhere on the Internet.

There are many types of products and services on the internet. However, how do you know to make the right choices when you have no idea about the reputation of the seller? How do you find good deals? Such questions can only be answered by having the right online shopping skills.

Online Selling

The same is true now with online selling. Gone are the days of geographical limits.

When you do a garage sale you can do it locally, nationally, or even internationally. Through the power of the Internet you can sell almost anything online. It is really true that one man's junk is another man's treasure. Knowing the skills of online selling can help you earn extra money for something you may have otherwise trashed. Why let it go to waste?

Summary

You have been introduced to the seven essential tools and skills that you can easily learn. Everything begins with the Internet browser--the window to the Internet. With email, you can stay directly connected with others. Through social networking, you can connect and reconnect with friends & relatives and maybe even discover new ones. Texting can keep you connected when you have limited access. If you need information on a subject matter, Internet research skills can find it for you. Online shopping skills can come in handy when you need to purchase something. Finally, if you have things you no longer need, online selling skills can help offload them to those who need them.

These are seven essential tools and skills you can learn to use. Just keep an open mind and you will see.

The Internet Browser

The Internet browser is probably the staple tool of Internet technology.

This terminology may sound intimidating, to some, but it is all in how you think. If you think that you can learn how to do this then you will.

This chapter will explain why this tool is one of the essential Internet tools today and will provide crucial information to help you learn how to use it.

Introduction

In 1993, the first popular Internet browser was called Mosaic (http://goo.gl/W5J3Lp). As the Internet became more popular, new Internet browsers started popping up. In 1994, Netscape Navigator was released. The following year, Microsoft released Internet Explorer and the Opera browser was released a year later. In 1998, Netscape launched the Mozilla Foundation which later evolved into Firefox in 2004. In the meantime Apple released Safari in 2003. The latest Internet browser entry came from Google with Chrome, introduced in 2008. Today, Chrome dominates the Internet browser market.

Anyway, is it enough to know how to open a browser and type a web address (technically known as the URL--uniform resource locator) in the address field of an Internet browser?

The answer is "no". You will need a little more than that to adapt to the ever changing Internet landscape. The important things to remember are:

- Many Internet browsers exist
- Browsers sometimes need extensions (a.k.a. plugins) to work
- Many devices allow Internet browsing
- Use basic Internet searching syntax
- Some of the top search engines

Why the Need?

Before you get too deep into this, you need to know why the Internet browser is an essential tool.

Without the Internet browser, you will be limited to things within your geographical boundary and physical reach. You can probably survive without, but why not take advantage of what technology has to offer? After all, technology is here to make life easier and better for everyone.

The Internet has so much to offer that there are literally hundreds of things you can do through the Internet browser. An article at forlanda.net lists various things you can do on the Internet in your day-to-day life (http://goo.gl/3TgE1h).

Below are some of the obvious things your Internet browser can help you do:

- Research any topic on the web
- Find and get entertainment online
- Stay connected with family & friends
- Buy and sell things
- Look up businesses
- Pay your bills
- Get maps and directions

To some degree, other online tools and skills depend on the Internet browser. Due to the rapidly changing technology, your Internet browser will help you to adapt easily and to take advantage of the unlimited resources the Internet has to offer.

To start using an Internet browser, you need a device to run it on. The next section will discuss Internet browser devices.

Internet Browser Devices

You need to know that there are many devices than can run Internet browsers. The most prevalent ones are listed below:

- Microsoft Windows-based computer systems (e.g. HP, Dell, IBM, Gateway, Acer, Asus)
- Apple-based computer systems (Mac-based computer systems)
- Apple iOS (e.g. iPhone, iPad)
- Android (various tablets and smart phones)
- Amazon Kindle Fire
- Barnes and Noble Nook
- Google Nexus
- Samsung Galaxy Tab 3
- Chromebook (e.g. Acer, HP, Samsung, Toshiba)

There are more but this list covers some of the major market players. This just means that you can experience the Internet through many devices, with the freedom to choose the one that will work best for you.

If you do not have any of these devices, it is time to get one. If you do not have time to deal with general purpose computer operating systems like Windows or Apple's Mac (or you don't care to really know what they are), a good place to start is with a simple tablet computer. If you do not have an idea which tablet to get, a safe bet would be one of these handy and inexpensive 7" or 8" tablet computers:

- **Samsung Galaxy Tab 3** (this URL will get to a Google search result for "Samsung Galaxy Tab 3 8 inch": http://goo.gl/KXbUAV)
- **Google Nexus 7** (this URL will get to a Google search result for "Nexus 7": http://goo.gl/JjeI9X)

These devices are fast, responsive, and reliable for $250, give or take $20 as of this writing. Be advised that every year the prices generally go down and the feature list gets longer. To get the latest price, enter the shortened links (in parenthesis below) on your Internet browser's address field:

- Search for Samsung Galaxy Tab 3 8-inch (http://goo.gl/kLqEDt)
- Search for Google Nexus 7 (http://goo.gl/wuK5M6)

Another option is to get a Chromebook. For less than $199, you can get an Acer C720 Chromebook at Amazon.com (http://amzn.to/1jrugv1). If most of what will do is on the Internet, then this laptop is for you. It uses what is called ChromeOS—an Internet browser based computer operating system. Its battery life is anywhere from 6 to 9 hours, depending on usage. With the built-in keyboard, typing a message is easier than with a screen-based keyboard on tablet computers.

Internet Browsers

As stated before, there are many Internet browsers. What you have initially is dictated by the device you have.

Here is the breakdown for desktop computers as of May 2014. As you can see, if you have a desktop computer, most likely you already have Internet Explorer.

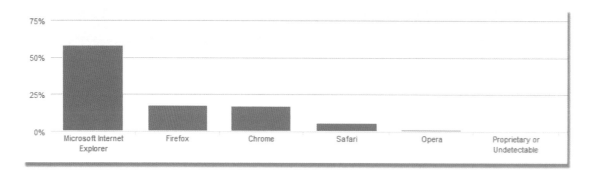

Here is the breakdown for mobile/tablet devices as of May 2014:

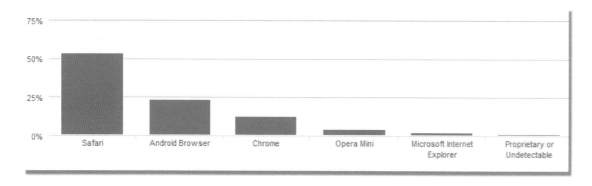

Reference: NetMarketShare.com Real-time Web Analytics for time range January, 2014 to April, 2014 (http://goo.gl/XOVJSL)

In the desktop computer platform, Microsoft Internet Explorer has the biggest portion of the market with both Chrome and Firefox a far second and third. For the tablet/mobile platform, the Safari browser (for iTouchs, iPhones and iPads) dominates with the android browser a far second.

In the combined market, however, the Chrome browser is dominant. For tablets and smartphones, Chrome is available as an app.

The author personally prefers Chrome over the other browsers as it has the ability to remember your user setup regardless of the device you use (provided you have a Google account).

Browser Extensions

Understand that browsers need a little help when content goes beyond images and text; this is where extensions (a.k.a. *plugins*) to browsers come in.

In the early years of the Internet, websites only showed text and images. However, since interactivity and media demand grew, browsers added extensions as a means of showing more dynamic content.

Today, the most common extensions include the following:

- Adobe Flash (http://www.adobe.com/products/flashplayer.html) - allows you to see most web animations and play games; Chrome already has this built-in
- Adobe Reader (http://www.adobe.com/products/reader.html) - required to read PDF (portable document format) files
- Adobe Shockwave (http://get.adobe.com/shockwave/) – used to play audio
- ActiveX (http://www.microsoft.com/security/resources/activex-whatis.aspx) - used to give Internet Explorer additional functions
- Silverlight (http://www.microsoft.com/getsilverlight/) - Microsoft's version of Adobe Flash

Missing one or more of these extensions may limit your ability to view rich Internet media content. HTML5 (http://goo.gl/Bnjq6g) is supposed to cure this extension dependency. As more application developers convert to HTML 5, Adobe Flash and Silverlight will be a thing of the past. All browsers support it, and many web sites (http://goo.gl/Y8468C) are already using it.

Basic Internet Searching

There are literally millions of websites out there. Below is a graph of the number of websites in the world as a function of time.

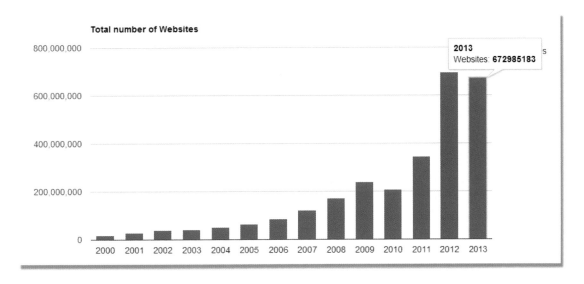

(source: http://www.internetlivestats.com/total-number-of-websites/)

In 2014, there are almost 1 billion websites.

With the numerous websites that cover topics from A to Z, you need an easy way to search the web. Through your Internet browser, your most basic searches will likely return millions of results. Who has time to sort through that!

This is when a better web searching skill comes in handy. I cover this skill in another chapter in detail, but what follows is just a good start for basic Internet searches.

First is the '+' or '-' qualifiers. If you use these in the search field of your Internet browser, it will help ensure anything with a '+' in front exists in the search result and anything preceded with a '-' will be filtered out of the search results.

For example, if you enter **+steak -chicken -eggs** in the search field, you will get back results that include the words "steak", and you will notice that none of the results have the word "chicken", nor the word "eggs," in them. Here's an actual example using Chrome to do a search through Google's search engine:

Google | +steak -chicken -eggs

Web   Maps   Images   Shopping   Videos   More ▼   Search tools

About 20,300 results (0.34 seconds)

Lindey's Prime Steak House, Restaurant and Bar, Casual ... ⊙
www.theplaceforsteak.com/ ▼
You will find Lindey's Prime **Steak** House nestled in woody Arden Hills, reminiscent of a
northern cabin from the 1950's; a unique atmosphere that is both casual ...
3.4 ★★★⯪ ★ · 29 Google reviews · Write a review · Google+ page

⦿ 3600 Snelling Ave N, Arden Hills, MN 55112
   (651) 633-9813

Restaurant Menu - Devon Seafood + Steak Oakbrook Terrace ⊙
www.devonseafood.com/menus.aspx?location_id=180 ▼
Devon Seafood + **Steak** in Oakbrook Terrace we have the freshest available seafood
direct from the most reputable sources on a daily basis.

THE Steak House - Circus Circus ⊙
www.circuscircus.com › Dining ▼ · Circus Circus Las Vegas ▼
The Best **Steak** House in Las Vegas for nearly 2 decades. Prime rib, lobster and crab
legs at affordable prices.

Vegas Strip Steak | The newest steak ⊙
vegasstripsteak.com/ ▼
There's nothing else quite like **steak** and it epitomizes the pleasure of eating beef. That's
what prompted a meat scientist, a chef and a university to team up to ...

(source: http://goo.gl/GUwl2h | the link on the left side will give you the search result using
+steak -chicken -eggs)

Notice that we end up with about 20,300 results. This is still a significant number. To further
narrow this down, you can search exact phrases by using quotation marks.

For example, if you want to search for "meat and potatoes" and not any permutation of the three
words like "and meat potatoes", then putting a quote on the three words in the order you want
them would do the job.

Specifically, using quotes to search for "meat and potatoes" the Google search engine returns
2,020,000 results. Without the quotes, the search comes back with 25,100,000 results. An

extremely significant difference.

Between the plus, minus, and quotes, you can pretty much narrow down your search results by orders of magnitude. Just give it a try.

Top Three Search Engines

Your Internet browser is set to use a particular search service by default. If you are using Internet Explorer for example, your default search engine (or service) is set to Microsoft's Bing.

There are other alternatives, and each will come up with a slightly different set of search results. Below are the top three search engines:

- Google
- Yahoo
- Bing

Although Internet browsers have one of these search engines as their default, you can change it. The author prefers Google's search engine as they have very good search results with a high degree of relevance. They periodically update their search algorithm to help continue improvements in returning very relevant results. If you are using Internet Explorer as your Internet browser, you can change the default search engine by following these steps:

1. Open Internet Explorer and type google.com in the address field.
2. If google.com isn't your default search engine, you will see this:

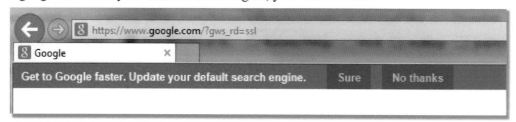

When you do, click **Sure**.

3. The Add Search Provider window will pop up.

Make sure to check the option for "Make this my default search provider," then click the Add button.

4. Google.com is now your default search engine on Internet Explorer.

Now back to the topic of search engines.

Here is a graph of the search engine market share in a May 28, 2014 article at http://searchengineland.com/recirculation-gap-192597.

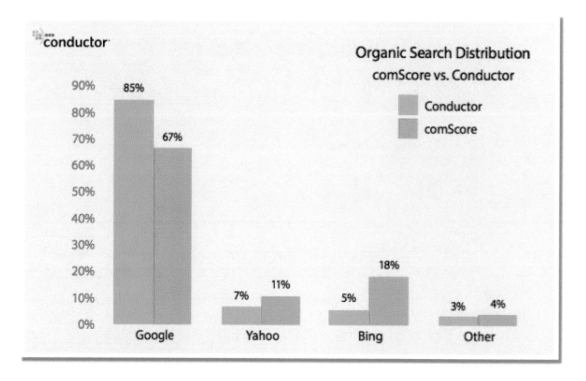

Regardless of which data source is used (Conductor or comScore), Google dominates the search engine market. Nevertheless, you can find almost all of what you need through one of the search engines.

Conclusion

You know that there are many things you can do through the Internet, and it is simply not enough to know how to open your Internet browser and surf. To take advantage of what technology has to offer, you start with your Internet browser. In addition, you also need to know:

- That there exist many other Internet browsers
- Internet browsers sometimes need extensions or plugins to work with certain Internet content
- That there are many devices upon which you can use an Internet browser to experience the Internet
- The basic Internet search syntax
- Which are the top search engines

If you understand the above, you have all you need to take advantage of your Internet browser and to adapt to the rapidly changing Internet landscape.

E-mail

Introduction

The "e" in e-mail stands for "electronic." E-mail (or email) has been around for almost as long as the Internet has been around. It is an essential Internet tool for the following reasons:

- It has staying power
- Almost everyone has an email address or can easily get one for free
- Almost everyone understands email addresses and have access to email services
- Email is easy to use
- Best of all, it is the staple communication tool for personal and business use

Staying Power

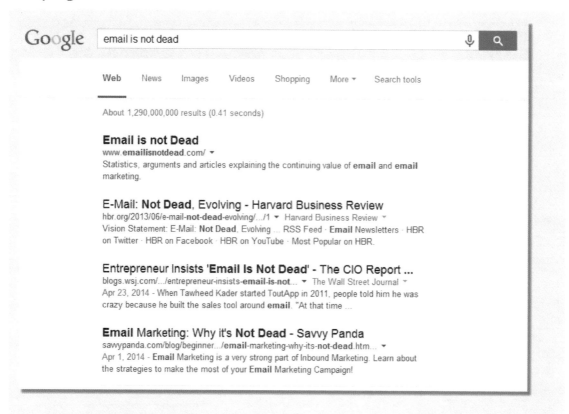

Email is not dead; search Google (or type this: http://goo.gl/5sJfG2 in the address field of your Internet browser) and you'll see.

A few years ago, people thought that email was dead when many started communicating using alternative means, like messaging via Myspace, Facebook, and direct texting. However, regardless of how many different ways there are in communicating over the Internet, email seems to withstand the test of time (**reference**: 22 Reasons Why Email Is not Dead by Christopher Knight, So No. Email is Not Dead. The Groupon Fail Proves It by Erika Morphy). After all, it has been around for over 15 years.

Everyone Has One or Can Get One Free

Long ago, before emails were common, people had to either subscribe to some Internet Service Provider (ISP), be attending some university, be part of a company who had their own email services, or be part of DARPA (http://www.darpa.mil/, Defense Advanced Research Projects Agency) in order to have email.

Today, as long as you have some access to the Internet, you can get yourself a free email address and services from the likes of:

- Yahoo.com (Yahoo mail)
- Google.com (Gmail)
- Live.com (Windows Live) (Hotmail)
- AOL (about.me)

Email services like Yahoo mail provide you email space that is practically unlimited.

Case in point...

I've had my yahoo and Gmail accounts for years (at least 10 years). I keep all my emails, yet never once did I get an alert about my mailbox being full even though I get hundreds of emails a day.

If you don't yet have an email address or you are still using your ISP's email address--like johndoe@sbcglobal.net, then it is time to get a new email address--one that you can keep regardless of who your Internet service provider is. The author recommends getting an email address from Yahoo.com or Google.com (Gmail to be exact).

For example, to apply for an email account from Yahoo.com, open your Internet browser and enter yahoo.com in the address field, and click the **Sign In** link once the Yahoo.com page shows up.

After that, you will see a new page that contains the login prompt. Click the **Create New Account** link.

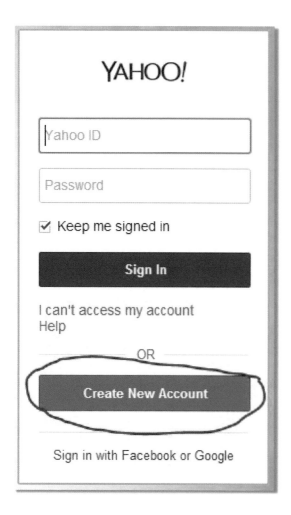

Just provide the required information. Note that the email account you choose may not be available, so keep trying to come up with one that you like and can remember. In the example below, I came up with the account itSensei@yahoo.com. Note that email addresses aren't case sensitive. Next, click the **Create Account** link.

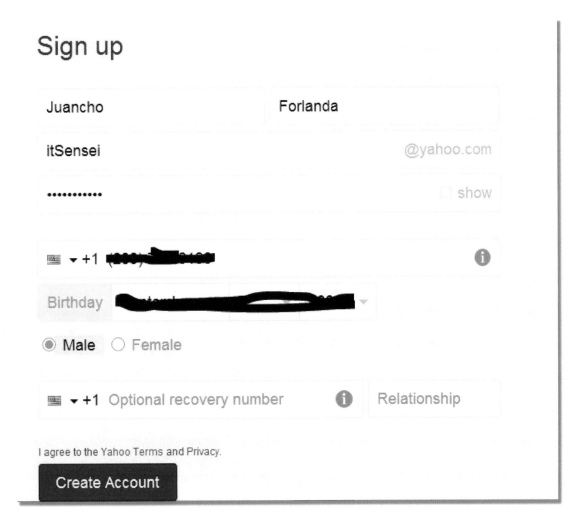

If there were no omissions or errors with the information you provided, you will see a verification page like the one below. This is called a CAPCHA verification code. In about one second you will get redirected to Yahoo.com to get started. Once at Yahoo.com, you can check your email by clicking the mail icon on the top right corner of the page.

Now you have an email address from Yahoo.com.

Almost Everyone Knows Email Addresses

Email addresses are well known to many. If you were to ask for someone about their email address, there is no need to explain what it is. They most likely have one the way they do a cell phone number. If, however, you are totally new to email and email addresses, here's how one looks like: itSensei@yahoo.com

Notice the "@" symbol. This delimits the unique email account (*itSensei* in this case) in the Yahoo.com system (or domain). The combination of the email account name and the system or domain name makes it unique on the Internet.

Anyway, most people know what email addresses are. As such, email makes it extremely easy to contact someone simply by knowing their email address. Gone are the days of paper mail; just send an email.

It is Easy to Use

Creating email is relatively easy. Provided you've already opened a new email to send, all you need to do is fill-in the following basic parts:

- **TO**: (required) the email address whose owner is to receive and take from this email
- **CC**: (optional) email addresses of people who are receiving courtesy copy of this email communication; this is optional
- **BCC**: (optional) email addresses who will get a copy of this email; the TO and the CC have no visibility into who is in the BCC list; the B stands for "blind"; this is optional
- **SUBJECT**: (optional) type a brief useful subject so that the reader will have a clue what the email is about; this isn't required, but having it is good practice
- **BODY**: (optional) the main message goes here; it isn't required, but if you want a useful email message, you should enter it here.
- **ATTACHMENT**: (optional) if you have a file you wish to send along, attach it;it isn't required

---

TIP: *Web-based email is the best way to take advantage of email. Client-based email programs like Outlook Express were common many years ago, but they require the need for configuration, and your emails get saved on your local computer storage device. If your computer breaks, so is your access to your email archives.*

Here's an example of how you compose an email using Yahoo's web-based email system.

First login to Yahoo.com and go into the email system by clicking the **mail** icon on the top right corner of the web page. From there, click the **Compose** link (see the following illustration).

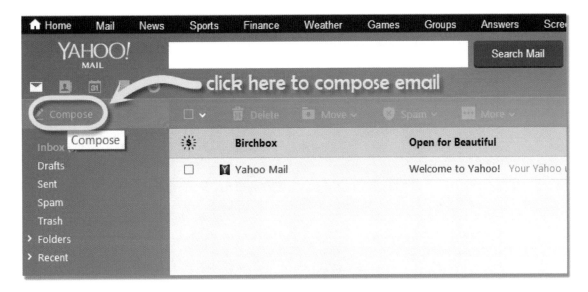

After clicking **Compose**, you will see this window. I've annotated it to show the different parts of the email.

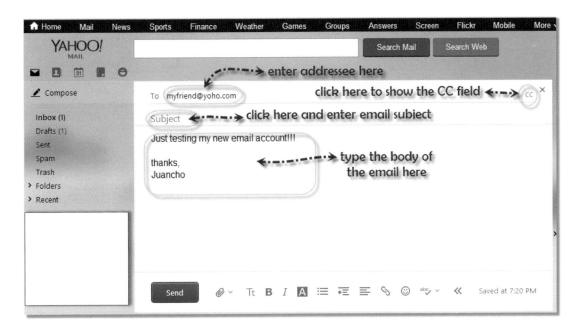

To begin composing email, you can click the Subject field of the email, then begin typing the subject of the message you intend to send. It should be something short but gives the recipient an idea what this email is all about.

Next, click the body area of the email, and begin typing your message.

Notice that we didn't click the **To** field yet. By not clicking the **To** field yet, we keep from accidentally sending the email with no or incomplete message. This sometimes can happen when we accidentally hit the **Send** button.

At this point though, the subject and body of your email is done. Now you are ready to specify who this email is for. Type the recipient's email address in the **To** field. If applicable, you can have more than one recipient. Recipients can be separated by a comma.

If you have to provide a courtesy copy of the email to someone, click the CC link, and you will see the CC field show up. You can then enter the email addresses of those you wish to receive a courtesy copy of your email.

If you wish to provide a courtesy copy of the email but don't want the **To** and **CC** recipients to know the email addresses of certain courtesy copy recipients, then click the BCC link, and you will see the BCC field show up. You can enter their email addresses in this field. When the To and the CC email recipients receive your email, they won't see the list of email addresses that you put in the **BCC** field. Thus, if the To or the CC recipients did a **Reply All** to your email, only the **To** and the **CC** addresses will receive the reply all message.

As you can see, creating an email is relatively simple. Once you get use to creating one, it will become second nature to you.

Staple Method for Personal/Business Communication

Communicating asynchronously is great. Unlike TEXTing, with email communication you aren't expected to respond right away. In most cases, people simply don't expect an instant response to their email message. Because of this, it makes for an excellent means for batch communication in both personal and professional applications. If you use email often, you should probably check it once or two times per day. Anymore and you incur some email administration overhead, which can eat into your productive time.

For personal use, people use email to:

- Apply or inquire about new positions or jobs
- Communicate or stay connected with friends and relatives
- Hold private and separate communication with people their digital social circles
- Send and receive consumer product support
- Send and receive payment (e.g. PayPal)
- Receive subscriptions or alerts for sites they've subscribed to
- Store various files (by the way, most web-based email services provide anywhere from 8GB and higher of space)

What is a GB (gigabyte)?

To understand the size of 1 GB, think of 1 byte as one character, like the letter "A".

In the computer world, there is a unit called KB or kilobyte. 1 KB stands for 1024 bytes. It is roughly a full page of text.

Next is the unit called MB or megabyte. In the computer world 1 MB is equal to 1024 KB. So 1 MB is over a thousand pages of full page text. Here's another point of reference--a fully digitized song can take about 5 MB of space.

Finally, there is the unit called GB or gigabyte. One gigabyte (1 GB) is equal to 1024 MB. Thus 1 GB is roughly equivalent to just over 1 million full pages of text.

As a side note...

There is a photo storage and sharing site call flickr.com. They offer free 1000 GB of storage for your pictures. That is a lot of space!

Gone are the days where one writes a letter and waits for the post office to deliver it. Email provides this free service at almost the speed of light! No more snail mail.

For professionals or businesses, use email for:

- Communicating to subscribers
- Marketing and promoting new products
- Receiving product and support inquiries
- Providing technical support and customer service
- Keeping customer base in the loop and maintain the relationship

When a company have to deal with thousands of clients, using email is the most cost effective means of maintaining relationships and doing product marketing.

Note that there are companies that specializes in this.

Such services help automate relationship management, marketing of products, customer service auto-responders, and so on--all through email.

The following are three of the most widely used email services on the Internet:

- Aweber (http://www.aweber.com/)
- Constant Contact (www.constantcontact.com/index.jsp)
- MailChimp (www.mailchimp.com) - free for up to 2000 email subscribers

There are no other electronic means of communication like email. It is versatile enough to use in both personal and professional situations.

Conclusion

At this point, you have to be convinced that email is indeed an essential tool in today's modern times for the following reasons:

- It isn't going out of style; it has been around for over 15 years and it will be for several more.
- Everyone has an email and if they don't they can get one free.
- Almost everyone knows and understands email addresses.
- Email programs, especially web-based are extremely easy to use.

- Last but not least, it is the staple method for communication in both the personal and business level. This is regardless of what's happening with Facebook and other latest Internet based social networking applications out there. I'm still using email and the companies I've worked with for the past decade continue to use them. I imagine email will continue to be the staple of Internet communication for some time to come.

Social Networking

Introduction

In the 21st century, it is only appropriate that better ways to connect with others become available for everyone to use. Am I referring to cell phones? No.

Today, everybody who uses the Internet is only a few clicks or taps away from connecting with another. It is simply amazing how fast and efficient making a connection to multiple people is today.

In this chapter, we will discuss why social networking is one of this century's essential tool. In doing so, we will cover the following topics:

- Definition of Social Networking
- Basic History
- Uses of Social Networking
- Common Social Networking Services
- Signing up for Facebook

After reading this chapter, you will be convinced and will probably realize other important things you can do with social networking.

What is Social Networking?

From the context of this book, "social networking" is the act of sharing information with a network of people who are within your reach through an Internet-based service, and where each person receiving this information could share the same with others in their network. The Internet-based service used here is not your typical web application, but is one which is designed for the easy and fast spreading of information.

When you are doing social networking, you are basically broadcasting information online to your network of friends or acquaintances. Or you could be following or subscribing to certain people or organization that are of interest to you. In which case, you receive periodic broadcast of information from them.

Why couldn't you do this using email? You could, but it isn't the same. The simple act of posting information within your social network status immediately conveys and spreads your ideas with ease. And since your friends can do the same, information can spread with viral speed! This is what makes "social networking" such a key tool in today's world.

And in today's world of mobile devices, people are social networking everywhere--at work, at home, while shopping, and even during vacation.

How Did It Come to Be?

Remember, we are social beings. On top of that, it is in our nature to share with others--whether it be personal or business in nature. With technology and the way it is evolving, it was certainly only a matter of time before someone figured out a way to socialize electronically in a very easy and efficient way.

Thus it was natural that facebook.com took off the way it did in February 2004, quickly building around 845 million active users 8 years later, in Feb 2012. Note that there are many other social networking services on the Internet, but most are special interest in nature, whereas Facebook is a general social networking service.

A more recent entry into the field is Google Plus (G+ for short). It first came into the scene in limited, invite only fashion in June 2011; then by September 2011, it became fully available to 18+ year old. It opened for younger kids in January 2012. As of this time, Google Plus was estimated to have 90 million active users. In September 2013, Google Plus surpassed 1 billion registered users! [en.wikipedia.org: http://goo.gl/gSxj47]

Twitter is another social networking service. It launched in July 2006. Through its micro-blogging feature of limiting postings to 140 characters (called tweets), it has garnered 300 million users as of 2011. This service generates over 300 million tweets and 1.6 billion search queries daily! [en.wikipedia.org: http://goo.gl/wmkZID] As of 01 Jan 2014, there are almost 700 million registered Twitter users [statisticbrain.com: http://www.statisticbrain.com/twitter-statistics/] .

LinkedIn (https://www.linkedin.com/) is another social networking service, with a focus professional connections. It was founded in December 2002, and was launched in May 2003 [en.wikipedia.org: http://goo.gl/jTp0Pg]. In 2006, they gained 20 million viewers, and by June 2013 they have acquired around 259 million users worldwide.

The ones mentioned above are the most prevalent and most influential at this time. However, there are many more services out there with specialized purpose.

What are Its Uses?

On the surface, these social networking services don't seem to have much use, except to announce to others your various activities or thoughts of the moment. Fortunately, there are many more uses for social networking than the casual user may realize.

The importance of social networking really is highlighted by the many things you can do with it for personal, professional, and non-profit purposes.

Personal Uses

- Stay connected with family & friends
- Find long lost family members or friends
- Meet new friends
- Create events and invitations
- Share photos and videos
- Keep abreast on topics or news you want to follow
- Use it as your personal resume
- You can use it as a source of income

Professional/Business Uses

- Product advertising and promotion
- Staying connected with customers
- Product/service announcements
- Customer lead generation
- Customer service
- Web site traffic generator
- Customer feedback
- Affiliate marketing

Non-Profit Uses

- Organizational promotion
- Stay connected with supporters
- Promote fundraising drives

Common Social Networking Services

Almost everyone knows Facebook. It is obviously "**the**" top social networking service out there. About 41.6% of the US population has a Facebook account! [en.wikipedia.org: http://en.wikipedia.org/wiki/Facebook]

Anyway, the number of social networking sites is many [en.wikipedia.org: http://goo.gl/QmIKum], but the ones that make or have potential of making the biggest impact are the ones below:

- **Facebook** (http://facebook.com) - general social networking service; "the" top social networking site on the planet
- **Google** + (https://plus.google.com/) - general social networking service; Google's response to Facebook
- **Twitter** (https://twitter.com/) - general social networking service; micro-blogging (each posting limited to 140 characters)
- **YouTube** (https://www.youtube.com/) - the top video sharing site on the planet
- **LinkedIn** (https://www.linkedin.com/) - social networking for professionals and businesses
- **Flickr** (https://www.flickr.com/) - photo sharing social networking service
- **StumbleUpon** (https://www.stumbleupon.com/) - bookmark sharing
- **Delicious** (http://delicious.com/) - bookmark sharing

Signing Up for Facebook

Since Facebook is the leading social networking service, and many people already have accounts there, it makes sense to start connecting using Facebook from the onset. In this section I'll show you how to sign up for a Facebook account.

1. With your Internet browser, go to www.facebook.com. Once there, you'll see a "Sign Up" section on the right side like the image below.

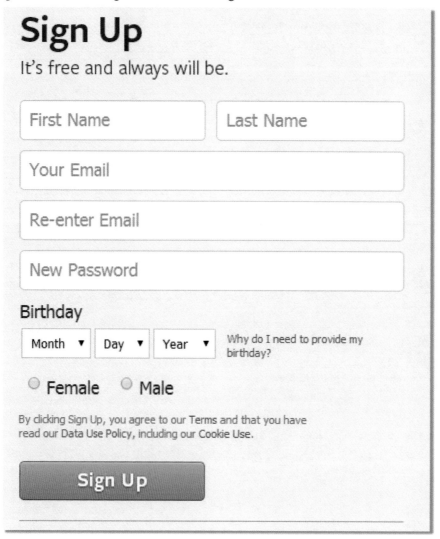

2. Just enter the information they request and click the **Sign Up** button. Below is an example of my entry using my Yahoo.com email account.

3. Upon successful sign up, you will see a window like the one below:

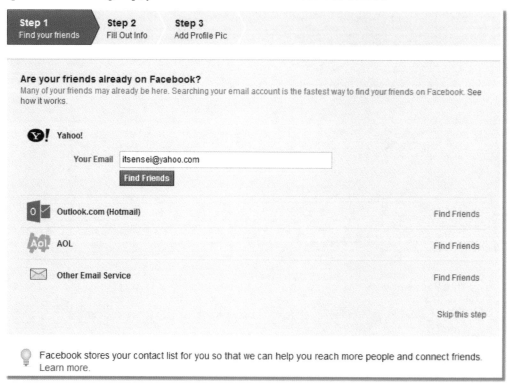

4. You don't necessarily need to start finding friends if all you want is to get your Facebook account established. So in this case, all you need to do at this point is click the "Skip this step" link on the bottom right corner of the page. It will ask you to confirm that this is what you want to do; so confirm it.

5. Next, Facebook wants you to provide more information about yourself. You can skip this as well by clicking the "Skip" link on the bottom right side of the page..

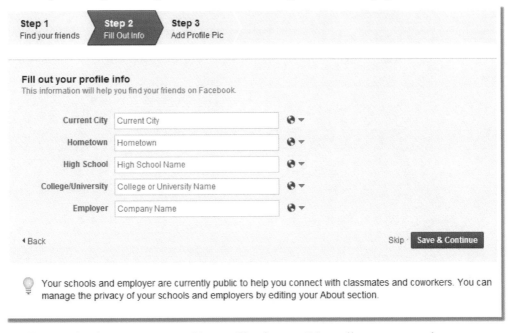

6. Finally, Facebook wants you to add a profile picture. It's really up to you what to put here. Just do it with tact. You can upload a picture or use the camera on your computer or device to capture one. Don't worry, this isn't permanent; you can change it at any time.

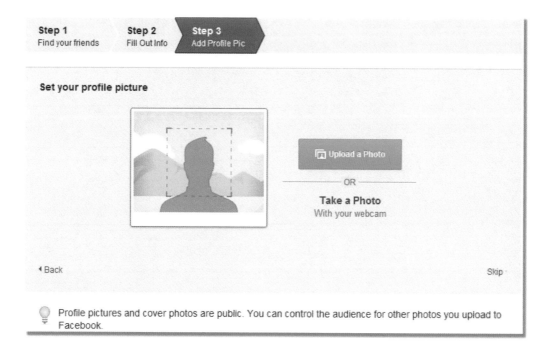

In my example, I uploaded an image. As you can see, my picture is a blurry image someone running.

All I need to do now is simply click the **Save & Continue** button.

7. You're almost done. At this point, Facebook will put you in your facebook.com home page, but you will need to check your email for a confirmation email which was sent by Facebook to the email address you provided during registration. Open that email and click the link that says **Confirm Account**, and you will get this:

Just click the **Okay** button and you are all set. You now have a Facebook account.

8. **But wait!!!** When connecting with friends and relative on Facebook, it is best to keep what you post there only visible to them. To do this, click the padlock icon pointed to by #1 in the image below. Thereafter you will see details about your privacy settings. In this case, the most important thing you want to check is what's pointed to by #2--"Who can see my stuff?" The answer to that is shown by #3. In this case, it shows "Friends." In general, this should suffice, but you must be selective about who you accept as friends, as they will see every post you make on facebook.com.

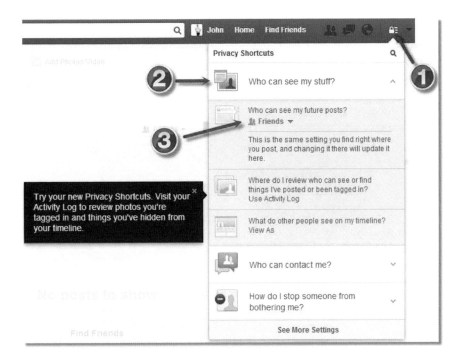

If you wish to limit visibility of your posts to your family and relatives, you may opt to create a custom group by clicking the arrow that points down underneath the question "Who can see my future posts?" and to the right of "Friends." It will pop up the following options:

In this case you'll have to select "Custom" and the following window then pops up:

In the Custom Privacy window, you can select specific people or lists who you wish to share with and also identify certain people who will not be allowed to see your posts. Don't worry. This is just the default settings for privacy. Every time you post, you can specify which list you wish to share your post.

That's it! You are good to go with Facebook social networking. Now go find your long lost relatives and friends!

Conclusion

Although on the surface it may not seem that social networking is important, the reality is...it is! There is no avoiding it. It is out there, wherever you go. People stay connected with their laptop, smart phone, and tablet. Its many uses really is what makes it one of the most important tools of the 21st century.

You can use social networking in your personal and professional life. You can even do the same for non-profit organizations. Through social networking, everyone is no further than a couple of clicks or taps away from everybody else. And through this, information and ideas can travel with great speed to those connected!

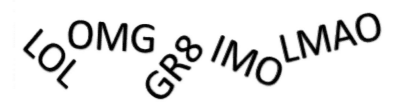

Texting

Introduction

Is TEXTing (or SMS – short messaging service) really an essential Internet tool? In this day and age, you most certainly need this tool in order to squeeze your message into small textual abbreviations when using your cell phone, or any other device where typing isn't easy to do.

Keep this in mind: this tool may go out of style when technology evolves to the point you can talk to your cell phone and have your message sent without any additional hand manipulation to fix and send that message.

That said, why is really TEXTing an essential Internet tool? The truth of the matter is, there will be occasions when the only service available to you for communication is your phone's TEXT service. When that time comes, you will be happy to know you have TEXTing available at your disposal.

Recently, there has been significant development in the use of TEXTing for secondary security for your various online accounts, like facebook.com and yahoo.com just to name a couple.

Let's get down to specifics of TEXTing importance:

1. It is simple and direct.
2. It is very compact.
3. It is the communication means of last resort.
4. It can provide a means for keeping your online accounts secure!

Simple and Direct

TEXTing is so simple that your grandma can do it. That simplicity is what makes this means of communication so popular.

When you want to send a text message from your phone, you simply push a function button or icon somewhere on the cell phone to initiate the texting process. The text editing view comes up and you can start texting away. When done, you simply enter the phone number (or select from a contact list) of the receiver and press the SEND button, and you're done!

On older and basic cell phones (see image), the keypad only has the standard sequence of numbers, including the * and # symbols. The 26 letters of the alphabet are mapped to the keypad. On most basic cell phones, the mapping goes as follows:

- 1 - punctuation marks
- 2 - abc
- 3 - def
- 4 - ghi
- 5 - jkl
- 6 - mno
- 7 - pqrs
- 8 - tuv
- 9 – wxyz

Basic Cell Phone
Image courtesy of Teerapun/FreeDigitalPhotos.net

Most cells phones use a patented predictive text technology called T9 (http://goo.gl/YGwfp7) so that as you press the keys that represent the letters of the word being entered, the cell phone guesses what word you are trying to enter and tries to complete it for you. This can be a convenience or a curse. Have you experienced a case where you quickly sent a text and seconds later realized that the predictive text decided to use a word you didn't intend? Then you know what I mean. If you are new to TEXTing, this is something to watch out for.

On newer cell phones, especially smart phones, the phone comes with either a slide-accessible keyboard in QWERTY layout, or an in-screen keyboard on cell phones with bigger or larger touch screens.

Very Compact

Texting can be very compact especially if you know many of the shortcuts or abbreviations to some of the most common words.

When time is of the essence, short compact messages can be entered and sent fast!

Here are some of the common abbreviations:

- OMG - Oh my god
- LOL - Laughing out loud
- IMO - In my opinion
- C - See
- D - The
- R - Are
- U - You
- L8R - Later
- LMAO - Laughing my ass off
- XOXO - Hugs and kisses

There are hundreds of these abbreviations. You can find them at Webopedia (http://goo.gl/EFDphr). There are also translators that can help you convert normal English text to TEXT lingo; and there are translators that take the TEXT message and convert it to English:

1. Text Slang Translator (http://www.noslang.com/) - translates TEXT to English
2. Englih to Text (http://transl8it.com/) - translates English to TEXT, and vice versa.

You can see how compact TEXTing can be from the example below:

- **Original message**: *See you later*.
- **Converted to TEXT**: *C U l8r*.

We went from 14 characters (including spaces and the period) to 8 characters including spaces and the period. This is a major reduction in size. If for some reason your text service has limitation on the number of texts you can send, this could save you a few bucks; or maybe it is time to get a new and more cost effective cell service with unlimited text service.

Communication Means of Last Resort

The voice and data services network are totally separate from the TEXTing service or network. Most people find that although they cannot make a normal phone call, they can still TEXT from their cell phone.

In a major emergency (e.g. the 9/11/2001 terrorist attack) most people will have difficulty making a phone call primarily because the voice network is congested, but because TEXTing uses a different path and is extremely lightweight, you can generally TEXT someone even if you can't call them.

The article below from FCC.gov clearly states this.

FCC.gov, Understanding Wireless Telephone Coverage Areas (http://goo.gl/dCRcTc)

"Emergency Situations

Some people purchase wireless phones for emergency use only. These people rely on their wireless phones as a vital means of getting help during personal and other emergencies. Remember that during widespread emergencies, the calling volume in particular geographic areas can increase significantly, and a wireless phone call may not go through. When call volume is high and capacity is limited, consider sending a text message. Text messages require much less capacity, so they may go through even if a voice call cannot."

Provides a Means for Securing Your Online Accounts

Several online services, including banks and email service providers give users the option to use their cell phone's texting capability as a means to verify that you are the user you claim to be. In Facebook.com for example, you can use your cell phone to ensure that no one can steal your login name and password and use it on a machine you've never used before. To do that, they would need your cell phone. To set this security on your Facebook account, do the following:

Secure Your Facebook Account

Click the down arrow next to the security padlock and then click **Settings**.

Then click Security. See image below.

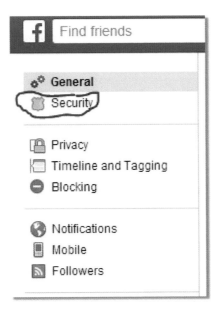

This brings you to the page below. Here, you can click the **Edit** link next to the line that says **Login Approvals** under Security Settings.

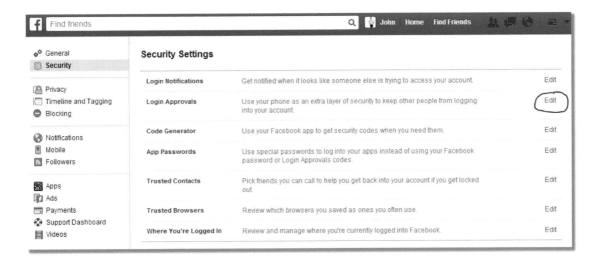

This will expand the Login Approvals section. Next check the option that says "**Require a security code to access my account from unknown browsers**."

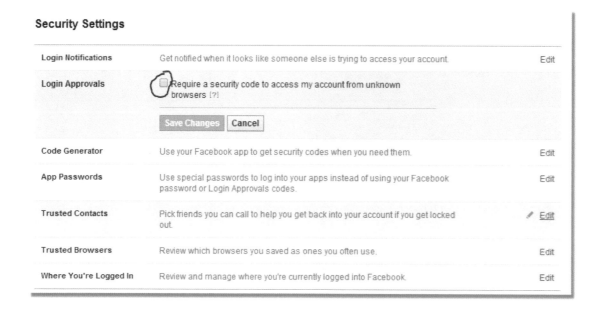

After you save changes, you will get informed about **What are Login Approvals**. Just click **Get Started**.

You then get the window below. Just select "Other" and it will prompt you for your cell phone. It will then text you a code which you will have to enter at this point to confirm that you own that cell phone. After entering the code, Facebook will, from here on, ask you to enter a code which it will send to your cell phone when you or someone tries to login to your account from a device you haven't used before.

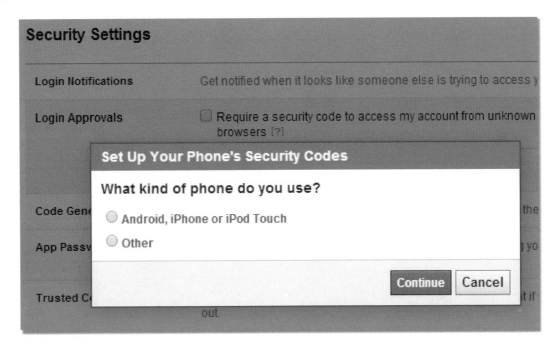

Secure Your Yahoo Account

You can do the same thing for your Yahoo.com email account. Simply click the gear icon on the top right corner of your Yahoo page.

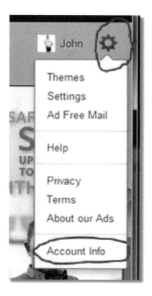

Next click the **Account Info** link. It will take you to this page.

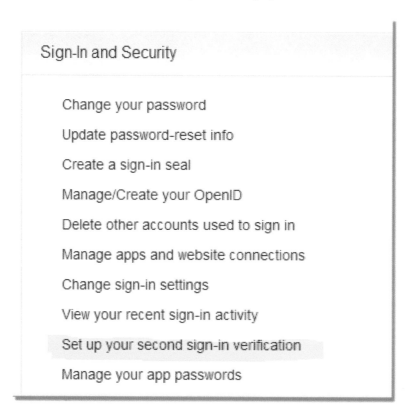

From here, click **Set up your second sign-in verification**, and it will begin the process of protecting your account. To begin, click **Get started**.

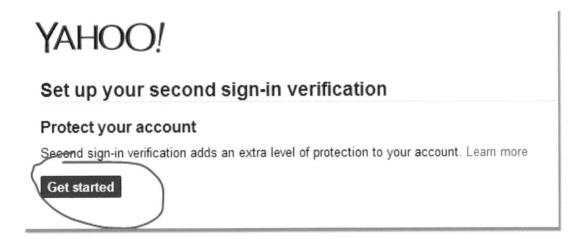

If you already specified a cell phone number in your profile, you will get this window; otherwise, you will be prompted to add a cell phone number.

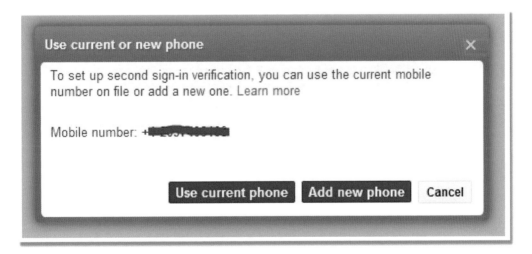

You can either use the current number, or add a new number. Once you set your cell phone number, you will arrive at this window:

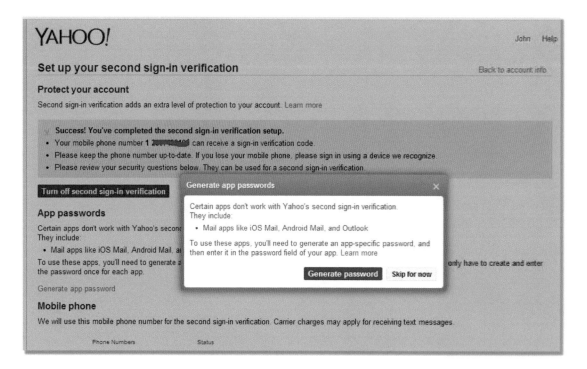

It basically says the you have set up your second sign-in verification, and that you may have to generate an app password for your cell phone, if you use an app in your phone which don't work with Yahoo's second sign-in verification. So basically, you'll need to generate an app specific password. You can click **Generate password** now or **Skip for now** depending on what you wish to do at this time.

If you generate a password, you'll get this.

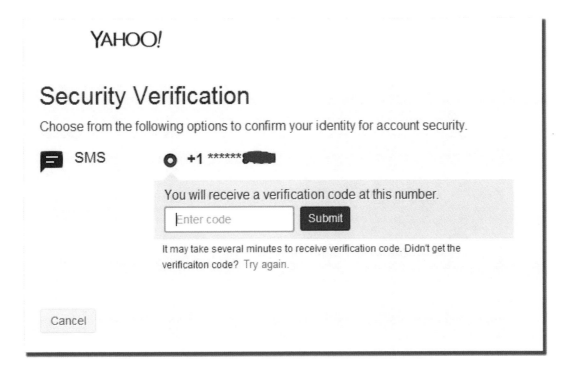

You'll get a code TEXTed to your cell phone. Enter the code and click **Submit**. Once you finish this, you will be taken back to the login prompt.

After logging in, you will see this:

At this point, you can specify an app name and then general a password by clicking **Generate**

password it will return a long alphanumeric string which you will use to help your app connect to your Yahoo.com account.

Conclusion

Although it isn't safe to TEXT and drive, TEXTing by itself can be considered an essential Internet tool. For one, TEXTing is simple and direct. Next, through TEXTing, you can send messages in a very compact way. Also, it can be the last means of communication if all else fail. Last but not least, You can use it to secure your online accounts.

Internet Research

Introduction

In today's world, almost anything is accessible to you via the Internet. As such, you have the potential for learning anything about any topic. All you need is a web-capable device like a tablet, laptop, desktop computer, Chromebook, or even your smart phone, and you are pretty much set. What a great and exciting time we live in!

This brings us to you. You want or need to learn about something? Do a search on the web and it comes back with millions of hits. Note that a "hit" is equal to one web page that may have the information you are looking for. Anyway, who has time to sift through all these? Let say you take 1 minute to sift through a hit. For 1 million hits, this would take you just about 695 days of continuous reading 24 hours a day with no sleep for almost 2 years.

There is just way too much information to sift through. How does one deal with the millions of possible sources of information to hasten the search for good and useful content? The answer is to have the necessary know-how for Internet research using your search engine (in this case we'll use Google's search engine) through your Internet browser.

To put this into better perspective, I will give examples of Internet research to solve specific problems of day-to-day challenges. To this end, I will cover these areas:

- Basic Internet search
- Advance Internet search
- Looking for Job
- Best way to lose weight
- Best way to earn money online
- Finding the best deals

Note that I will not cover how you actually do these things, but what you need to do to help narrow down the search in a manageable way. Again, the goal is not to find all information about a topic, but to find the few and useful relevant content applicable to your topic. We want to do it quickly and efficiently. That is our goal.

Basic Internet Search

We covered some basic notion of Internet search on the chapter that covered Internet browsers. This section will expand on this.

Most people don't know that there exists many search engines out there. You may have a favorite, but in this article we will focus on Google's search engine. Google, whether we like it or not, is the still the leader in the Internet search market [Jun 2012 - Updated // Search Engine Market Share (http://goo.gl/vtiW4F), karmasnack.com], with Yahoo and Bing coming in at a far second and third, respectively.

As such, all search syntax here will be focused on Google searches.

Just Search

On any browser, when you type something other than a web address, the browser assumes you are doing a search. The words you put there are used as part of the search criteria. By default, the browser assumes that any content that has all of the words you typed in meet the criteria. Using Google Chrome (my favorite browser), I show how it assumes you are doing a search.

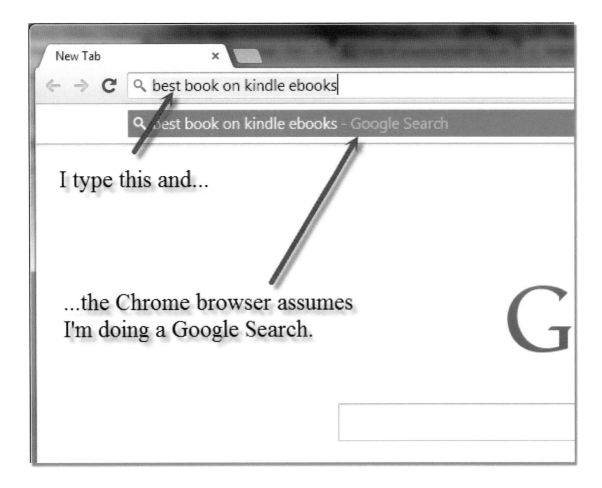

Here's an example of a straight search. if you simply put these words as your search terms: **basic internet search techniques**, your browser will come back with over 40 million hits. This isn't bad since Google tries its best to put the best sites at the top of the organic search results. The term "organic" here means that the returned hit isn't one that is a paid for ad from some online business looking to make a sale on a subject matter you may be looking for. Anyway, if you're lucky, you don't have to go any further than this. By the way, the search isn't case sensitive; so you don't have to worry about making sure you have the correct case settings.

Remember, this search means that if the search engine finds the words **basic**, **internet**, **search**, and **techniques** anywhere on the site, it will consider it a hit, regardless of the order in which they come.

Most people are happy with their search results using this very basic search technique; but, let's just say this didn't result on hits that are relevant to your search. What do you do then?

Narrowing Down the Search

We won't get too fancy in narrowing down our search here, but what I will explain will suffice for most search needs.

The first and easiest thing is to use existing tools that Google search provides.

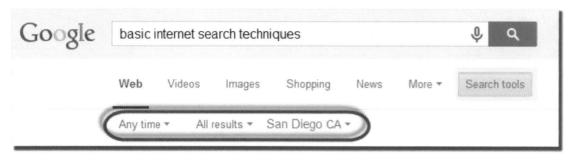

As you can see above, just below the search field, I've highlighted the link to **Search tools**. If you click that, you will get what I've circled in red above. You can use these to help narrow down your search.

If you click the arrow that points down next to "**Any time**," it will show you the options shown below:

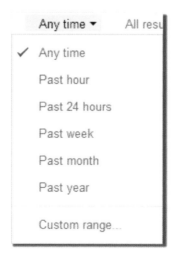

This can help narrow down your search to a time range that interests you.

The next field that can help narrow down the search is the one with the text "All results."

The value that makes the most sense to use here is to select **Verbatim**. This will return results that include the words you entered in the exact sequence you entered them. In this particular example, the search results came back with about 7 million hits--a significant improvement from 40 million hits.

The last search filter provided by the search tool is location specific. If what you are searching for is geographic in nature, you'll probably include a location as part of the search filter for say a search for a steak and lobster restaurant. The search option would look like this:

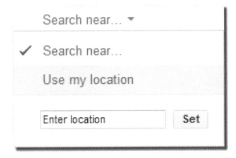

The default is "Search near...." And if your device or computer is allowed to report its location, this may just meet your needs; otherwise, you can specify an more exact or different location.

Advance Internet Search

Sometimes the results we are getting from a search may still be overwhelming in count. To get down to the most relevant search results, you'll need to apply some advance search techniques. This includes the use of the following:

- Exact phrase search
- Search within a website

- Exclude terms
- Wildcards
- OR operator

Exact Phrase Search

When you want to search for something very specific, do it using exact phrase. To do this, you need only enclose your phrase with quotes. For example if you put **"miniature white ponies"** in the search field (including the quotes of course), this tells the search engine to literally look for only sites that have this phrase. So be careful when using this search technique since it is very literal.

Since it is very literal, you can use this technique to also search for sites with words "as is". Remember, sometimes Google might try to help you out by assuming synonyms for things you are searching for. A good example is a search for the term **blackbelt**. Without quotes Google will also come back with results including sites that mention **black belt**. If that isn't what you want, exact word search using quotes will do the job.

Search Within a Website

On occasion, you might already know the content to be at a particular site. This is when searching within a website comes in handy. The syntax for this is as follows:

```
[search term(s)] site:[web site].
```

For example, if you are looking for some content related to boxing at yahoo.com, you would put this in the search field: **boxing site:yahoo.com**.

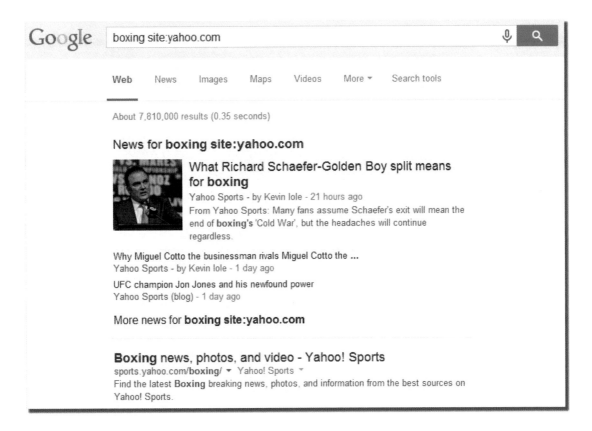

Supposing that you are doing a search for boxing at all .com sites, the syntax for this would be:

```
boxing site:.com
```

This would scour all .com sites for the topic "boxing".

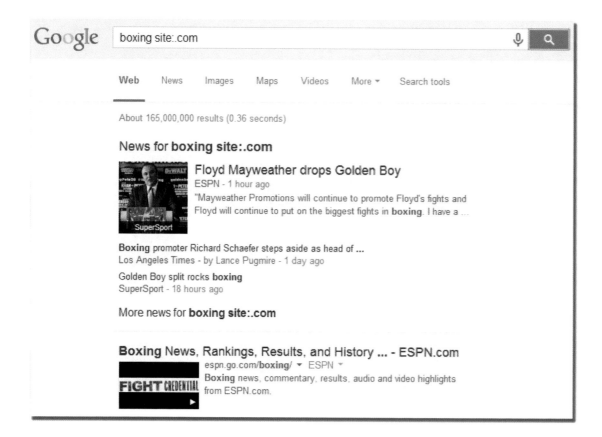

Keep in mind that the `[search term(s)]` portion can take any search string; so you can get pretty fancy with searches within web sites.

Exclude Terms

Under certain situations, you may want to exclude certain terms from your searches because you know it will result in hits that are irrelevant. For those rare cases, you can use the hyphen or minus character (-).

For example, if you are searching for information about dogs but don't want anything related to bulldogs, you would do a search using this search string: `"training dogs" -"bulldogs"`.

This would look for all contents that literary discuss "training dogs" because it is quoted, and it will exclude any content that has the literal term "bulldogs".

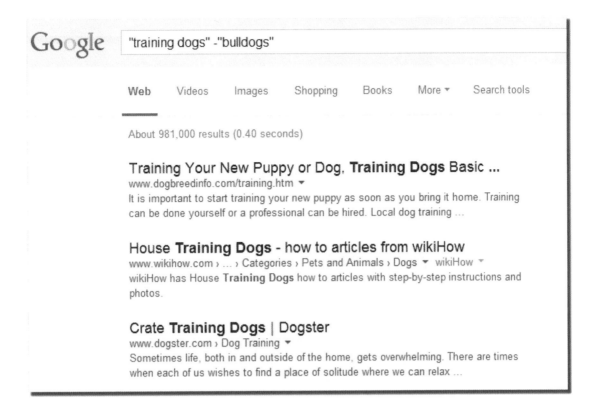

Wildcards

When you are looking for a topic with some kind of pattern, you can use the wildcard character-- the asterisk (*). Here's how it can come in handy. Supposing you are looking for all boxing opponents that Muhammad Ali had. To search for this, use this search string: **Muhammad Ali versus ***. This will come back with information specific to Muhammad Ali and his various boxing matches in the past or comparison of Ali with other boxers even in the present.

After pressing ENTER you will get this:

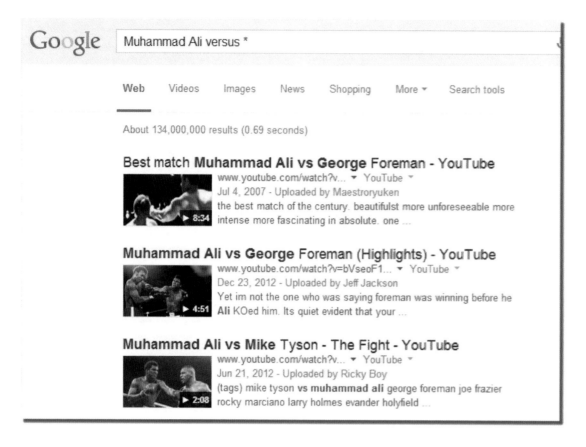

The bottom entry of the search above is obviously a comparison of Ali to Tyson since they are generations apart in terms of their boxing career. Nevertheless, it fits the pattern.

OR Operator

Searches using a string of words are by default separated by the AND operator. In other words, if you are searching for the term **brown dog**, the search engine inherently assumes you are searching for sites with the terms "brown" AND "dog" in it. Both words have to exist in order for a site to qualify to be part of the search result.

In order to use the OR logic you need to explicitly put OR between the words or literal words where you wish to apply the operator.

For example, if you are looking for the San Francisco 49er 1981 or 1982 records, you would enter the following strings: **San Francisco 49er 1981 OR 1982 records**. The OR will apply to 1981 and 1982. So any sites that have the following sets of words in its content will meet the search criteria:

- San, Francisco, 49er, 1981, records
- San, Francisco, 49er, 1982, records

The actual results below confirms that the OR function worked as expected.

Google   San Francisco 49er 1981 OR 1982 records

Web   Shopping   Images   News   Videos   More ▾   Search tools

About 378,000 results (0.44 seconds)

1982 San Francisco 49ers season - Wikipedia, the free ... ⊙
en.wikipedia.org/wiki/**1982_San_Francisco_49ers**_season ▾ Wikipedia ▾
The **1982 San Francisco 49ers** season was the team's 33rd in the league. ... **1982 San
Francisco 49ers**; ^ NFL 2001 **Record** and Fact Book, Workman Publishing ...
Personnel - Staff - Regular season - References

1981 San Francisco 49ers season - Wikipedia, the free ... ⊙
en.wikipedia.org/wiki/**1981_San_Francisco_49ers**_season ▾ Wikipedia ▾
Jump to Awards and **records** - [edit]. Joe Montana, Super Bowl Most Valuable Player;
Bill Walsh, National Football League Coach of the Year Award.
Offseason - Personnel - Regular season - Postseason

1981 San Francisco 49ers Statistics & Players - Pro-Football ... ⊙
www.pro-football-reference.com/.../**1981**.h... ▾ Pro-Football-Reference.com ▾
Super Bowl XVI Champs over Bengals, 13-3 (po:3-0), , ProBowl: Dean(), Hicks(), Lott(),
Montana(), Cross(), Clark()

1982 San Francisco 49ers Statistics & Players - Pro-Football ... ⊙
www.pro-football-reference.com/.../**1982**.h... ▾ Pro-Football-Reference.com ▾
1982 San Francisco 49ers ... Scored 209 points (23.2/g), 7th of 28 in the NFL. 49,
Earl Cooper, 25, FB, 9, 5, 24, 77, 0, 9, 3.2, 8.6, 2.7, 19, 153, 8.1, 1, 20, 2.1 ...

1981 San Francisco 49ers Roster - The Football Database ⊙
www.footballdb.com/teams/**nfl**/san-francisco-**49ers**/roster/**1981** ▾
San Francisco 49ers. NFC West - 2013 **record**: 12-4 ... **1981 San Francisco 49ers**
Roster ... Saladin Martin, DB, --, --, 01/17/1956, San Diego State. Milt McColl ...

49ers Year-by-Year: **1982** - Niners Nation ⊙
www.ninersnation.c... ▾ Niners Nation :: Unofficial San Francisco 49ers Blog ▾
Apr 10, 2009 - A brief historical recap of the **San Francisco 49ers**' **1982** season - a ...

Looking for a Job

Let us put our search engine tool to use in looking for a job. Let's say you are looking for a position as a Sales Manager. In addition, let's say you want to limit the job search to cities in the Central Valley, California--like Lodi, Stockton, Manteca, Tracy, Ripon, or Modesto.

To do this, you would enter the following search strings:

"Sales Manager" Manteca OR Stockton OR Lodi OR Tracy OR Modesto OR Ripon

Here's how this string breaks down.

The first part-- "Sales Manager" -- says that you are looking for must have the literal phrase "Sales Manager" in it . And, it must have one of the following cities: Manteca, Stockton, Lodi, Tracy, Modesto, Ripon. The following image is the result--over 2 million hits.

You obviously need to narrow down the search to more relevant results. Use the search engine's search tool to help with this by narrowing the search to only return results posted within the past week. This results in about 7,000 hits:

Say for example you are interested in a Sales Manager job in a car dealership. Add this to the search string: "car dealership." This brings the results down to just around 100.

About 100 results seem realistic enough as a good starting point to sort through potential jobs.

Notice that had you started sorting through the jobs when the results came back with over 2 million, you would be wasting hours just figuring out which is relevant and which is a good lead.

Best Way to Lose Weight

Oh, you say you want to figure out how to get to your ideal weight? Let's use the search engine to find out the best way to lose weight. We all know "best way to lose weight" is such a broad topic that it can result in millions of hits--at the time of this search I found over 100 million hits for the terms that include the words: best way to lose weight.

Let's narrow this down further by including "healthy food" and exercise to our search. Now our search string looks like this: **best way lose weight "healthy food" OR exercise**. As you can see in the image that follows, this reduces the hit result to just about 61 million hits. A major improvement, but still in the millions!

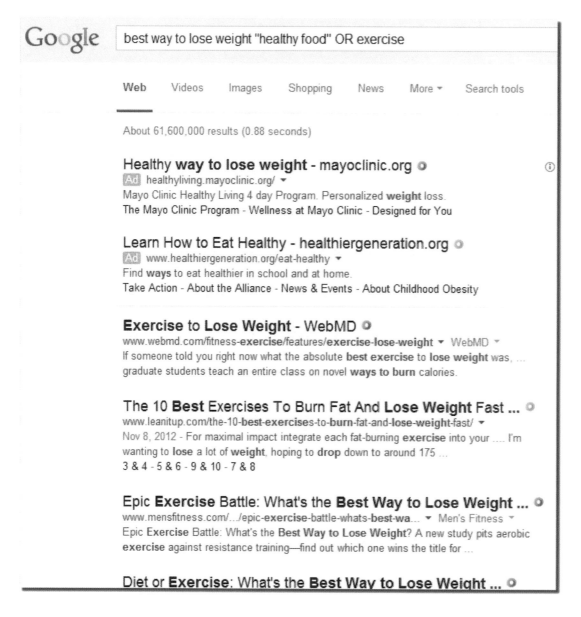

Also, let's make "best way" to be an exact phrase; so now our search string looks like this: "best way" lose weight "healthy food" OR exercise. These simple changes narrowed down the search down to 13 million hits. A major improvement, yet still extremely significant count to sort through.

This is still way too many to wade through. Let's get even more specific. Let's change "exercise" to "running", and let's add "water", "fruits", "flat tummy", and "for men". All these are sufficient to help narrow down the search.

The new search string now looks like this:

```
"best way" lose weight "healthy food" OR running water fruits
"flat tummy" "for men".
```

This trims down the search results to about 650 hits.

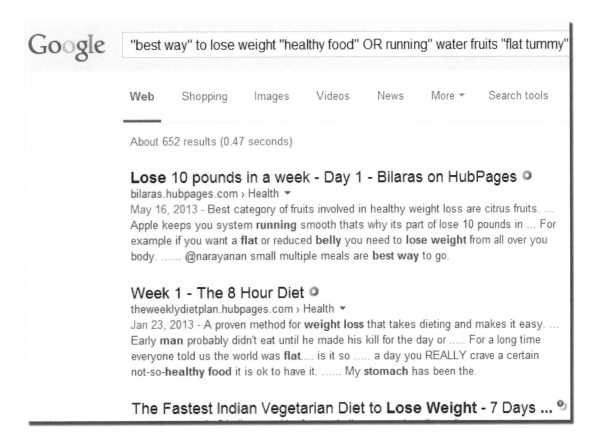

As you can see, you can bring your search results down to something manageable by realizing the proper use of search terms.

Best Way to Make Money Online

If you simply enter the strings "best way to make money online", you will get around 485 million hits! This is such a hot topic that there is so much content out there. Not sure which is good and which is bad, but who has time to go through hundreds of millions of web pages to try and figure out the best ways to make money online!

As usual, this calls for some serious narrowing down or modification of search strings. Try narrowing it down to these terms: `"make money online" "passive income"` `royalty "low startup cost"`. Below is what you get.

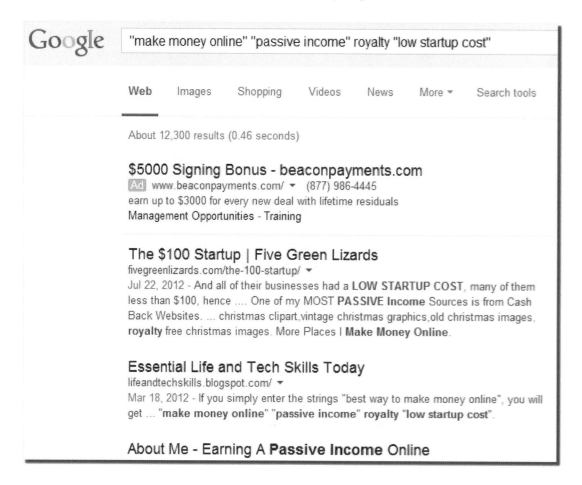

The best means to make income online is through passive income or get royalty payments. On top of that, the solution you find must have low startup cost. This new search string resulted in 12,300 hits. It is still a lot, but this is a popular topic on the Internet, and it is significantly better than the original 485 million.

Finding the Best Deals

Now-a-days you don't have to drive around to find the best deals. You can let your fingers do the searching online using Google's shopping tool. This is such an awesome tool that the best way to show how this works is by showing you. In the video below, I'm looking for the best deal I can find on a 60 inch LED TV which I can buy online. The HD version of this video (at http://youtu.be/l4BD60bH0Is) provides better viewing experience. Check it out when you get a chance. In the meantime, here are the steps you can take to find the best deal on say a 60" LED TV.

Google Shopping provides a vast array of options to help narrow down your search, to include:

- Price range
- Brand
- Product options
- Shipping (free or not)
- Review ratings

To begin finding that great deal, first go to Google's Shopping page. It is at https://www.google.com/shopping.

Next enter in the search field string "60 inch LED TV", as illustrated in the image, and press ENTER. You will get the following results:

As you can see, the right main panel shows your initial search results. The leftmost column shows your filter settings. Since the default is to show the most popular, you may opt to search using your own custom filter and sort order. The list of filter options available for TVs that are available to you are:

1. Geographic location (city and state)
2. Show only (in stock nearby, new items)
3. Price
4. Category
5. Brand (select one brand at a time)
6. Display type
7. Screen size
8. Number of HDMI ports
9. Depth
10. Weight
11. Features
12. Seller

Since you are looking for the best deal, let's adjust the filter to show Price of $500 or less for a Samsung brand LED TV. Ooops! That didn't get any hits. Let's clear the filter and adjust the search filter to set price of $1000 or less for a SAMSUNG brand LED TV, and sort the list from low to high.

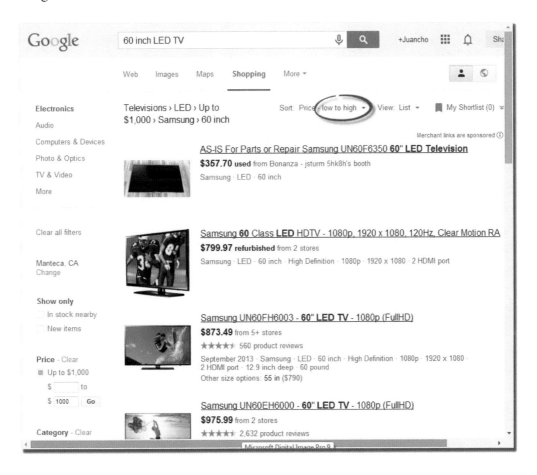

Looks like we found a deal for only $799.97. Here is the adjusted search filter:

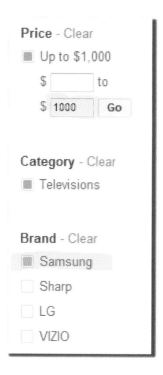

The sorting is handled by the sorting option here:

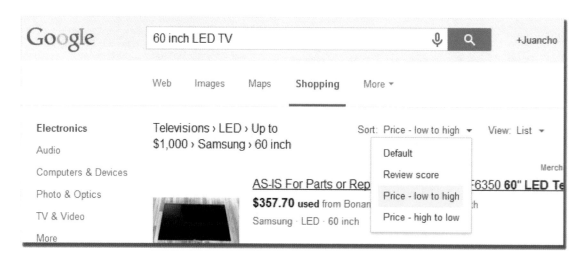

If you are happy with the result, then you've found the best deal. If you wish to purchase it, just click the link for that product and it will provide you with more details about the product, including the seller, and their rating. It even shows you the shipping charge.

The seller rating is an indicator of the buyers' satisfaction with the seller. Anything 4 stars or higher would be an above average seller that you can generally be happy about. There is one additional information provided here. It shows that the product for sale is "Refurbished." If you don't mind this, the product typically gets the same warranty as a new item; so it is like buying it new.

If there were other stores or sites selling this, you will see them listed below the top seller. In this case, there is only one other--Overstock.com. And as you can see, it costs $992.99 to purchase this type and brand of TV there.

Conclusion

In today's totally connected world, you need to take advantage of your search engine tool. There is such a vast library of knowledge out there ripe for the taking especially to those who are willing to take time to learn some basic and even advanced search techniques.

With search skills and your search engine, you can do many things:

- Find a job through the search power of the Internet
- Learn about the best ways to lose weight

- Discover the best ways to earn money online
- And find the best deals online

These are just examples; your only limit is your imagination.

This is indeed exciting times--a time when with just a few keystrokes, you can have at your fingertips information you need.

Online Shopping

Introduction

In today's Internet connected world, the paradigm for shopping has completely changed for the good. It's no longer a matter of looking for the latest best deals on the local newspaper ads, then going to the local store to buy that special deal. Instead, you can simply open your Internet browser and start shopping--7 days a week, 24 hours a day.

If you are still shopping the old fashion way, you need to read this--especially if you like finding good deals.

To get absolutely the best deals, you need to be aware of the following key things:

- You still need the brick and mortar stores
- The best way to determine the best price
- The Internet venues for online shopping
- Ways to determine if an online store is reliable or trustworthy
- How to compare prices
- The role of smart phones

You Still Need Brick and Mortar Stores (BaMS for short)

Even though you can buy almost everything online, you'll still need brick and mortar stores (BaMS). First of all, let's make sure we are all on the same page regarding the meaning of a brick and mortar store. These stores are places that take up real estate to show and sell products. Examples of these stores include Walmart, Target, and Best Buy. You also will find clusters of BaMS at shopping malls.

The good thing about BaMS is that when you find what you like, you can simply buy it and you get the item right there and then--no waiting for delivery. The bad thing is that it may not be the least expensive price. Most of the time, prices online are significantly lower.

Never the less, BaMS can serve a crucial purpose which no online stores can do. At BaMS, you can physically, see, touch/feel, taste (ask for a sample), and smell the merchandise. No picture or video can ever replace that experience your senses can only get from BaMS. Because of this, take advantage of BaMS to physically check out items before you get them online.

Sometimes BaMS may actually have the best deal. I've seen this happen during Black Fridays-- which now begins the same night as Thanksgiving at stores like Walmart, Target, and other retail stores. So keep an eye out at BaMS as well.

Determining Best Price

One of the best ways to figure out the best deals is through the use of Google's shopping tool (http://www.google.com/shopping). From there you can search for items you need.

Say for example you are in need of a new microwave oven. In the shopping tool's search field enter "microwave oven" and Google will come back with results based on relevance--i.e. most popular.

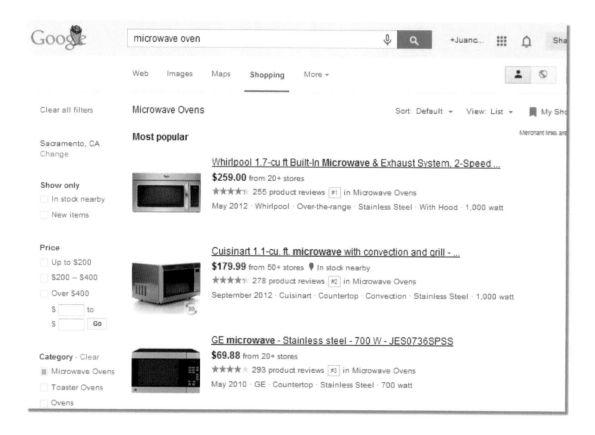

On the left hand side of the search, Google provides you with filtering options to quickly narrow down your search. The filtering options include:

- **Show only if**: in stock nearby, free shipping, and/or new items
- **Price**: any price, ranges of prices, or specify range
- **Brand**
- **Type** (for my microwave search, types were counter top or over the range)
- **Wattage** (this shows for microwaves, it shows particular attributes depending on the product)
- **Features**
- **Store** (if you prefer to look for it in a particular store, you can filter on this)

Price
- Up to $200
- $200 – $400
- Over $400
- $ [   ] to
- $ [   ] Go

Category - Clear
- Microwave Ovens
- Toaster Ovens
- Ovens
- Food Storage Containers
- Kitchen & Dining Carts

More

Brand
- GE
- Sharp
- Whirlpool
- Panasonic
- Frigidaire

More

Type
- Over-the-range
- Countertop

Wattage
- Under 900 watt
- 900 – 1,000 watt
- 1,000 – 1,100 watt

More

Type
- Over-the-range
- Countertop

Wattage
- Under 900 watt
- 900 – 1,000 watt
- 1,000 – 1,100 watt
- 1,100 – 1,200 watt
- Over 1,200 watt

Features
- Convection
- Sensor Cooking
- Stainless Steel
- With Hood
- With Removable Rack

Seller
- Sears Outlet
- Home Depot
- Walmart
- Overstock.com
- Abt Electronics & Appliances

More

Depending on what you are looking for, your search should quickly give you an idea on what a good deal should cost. From there, you should compare with what you see in the local area since sometimes **BaMS** send out ads to advertise their best deals.

Here's one I found by setting the following filters:

- **price**: up to $200
- **type**: countertop

I then set the sorting to **Review score**, and this is what showed as the top three best rated microwave oven for under $200:

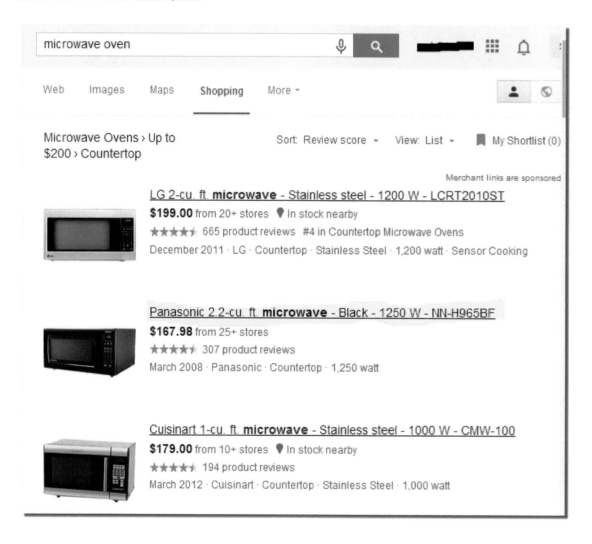

For my budget, I would probably get the Panasonic 2.2-cu. ft. Black 1250 W unit. It is the least expensive and has the highest power rating. When I click the link it shows this:

I can actually buy this at Walmart for the advertised price plus $14.28 in tax, and shipping is free. When I click the Walmart link, which I circled above, it takes you to the Walmart site.

Juancho Forlanda

At Walmart.com you can even watch a video of the product if you wished. If you're in a town with a Walmart, you can get the product shipped to your local store at no cost. They call this "**site** to store" delivery. If you aren't sure where the closest Walmart is, you can specify your Zip code, then click the **Find** button. When you do, Walmart.com will find all the Walmarts within 50 miles of your zip code, listing the closest one first. Identify the Walmart where you wish to have the product delivered by clicking the link that says Make This My Store.

Store Information	Pickup As Soon As	Choose Your Store
Walmart store #1840—Manteca 1205 S Main St	Mon 6/16 Need it sooner?	Make This My Store

Once you do this, you may get a helpful message from Walmart.com like this:

Shopping Walmart.com just got easier!
Here's what you need to know:

- You'll see items available for pickup with **site** *to store* at your Stockton store.

- When you checkout, we'll automatically choose Stockton as the store you want to pick up your items from.

- Changing your preferred store is easy! Just move your cursor over the **My Store** icon at the top of Walmart.com and follow the instructions.

Close

Just click Close and you are taken back to the microwave offer from Walmart. Just click **Add to Cart** when you are ready to purchase.

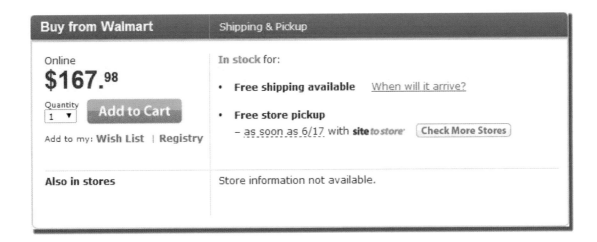

Walmart.com will ask if you wish to purchase additional warranty protection. Just opt out of it.

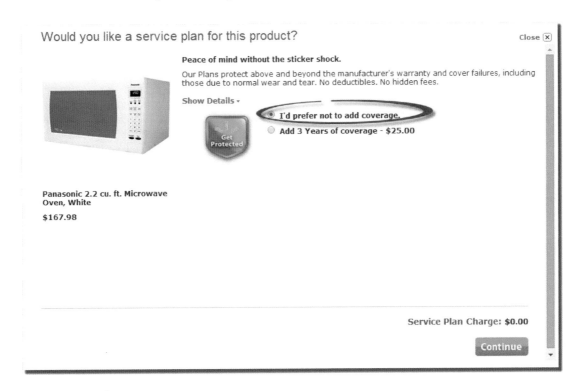

Click **Continue** and Walmart.com will provide you with a summary of costs before you can proceed to checkout.

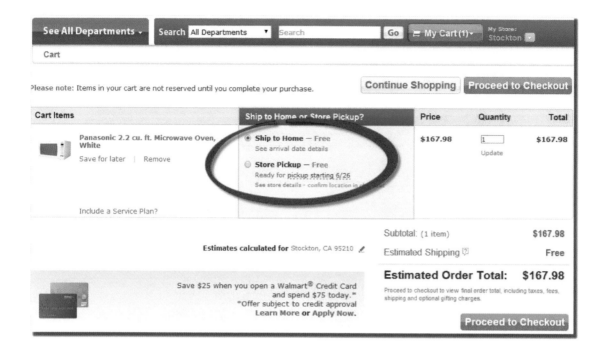

You still can opt to either ship it to your home or do a store pickup. In either case, the shipping cost is free. Choose whatever is convenient for you, then click Proceed to Checkout.

Now, each online store is going to be different in the purchasing experience. In all cases, your item(s) will end up on a cart, and you simply click **proceed to checkout** in order to finish the purchase.

Amazon.com

I've created a separate section on amazon.com. This online site is a major online shopping store. You can pretty much find anything at amazon.com at a fairly good price, especially if you are a Prime member.

At the time of this writing Prime membership costs $99 per year. If you are a Prime (http://goo.gl/gdTCo3) member, products that are designated as Prime will have special pricing with a 2-day free delivery. I am an Amazon prime member, and because I regularly purchase from Amazon, I recoup the annual Prime membership cost in no time due to shipping savings and special pricing for prime members. So if you aren't a prime member, consider being one and you'll also get access to their library of videos, music, and books.

Here are the advantages of purchasing at Amazon.com:

- Prices are generally pretty competitive, especially with Prime membership
- There are very useful product reviews. I typically use the product reviews to assess the quality of the product I'm about to purchase.
- Returning a product, if you are unhappy with it, is very easy. They even provide the return labeling which you can print during the online return request process. You just need to make sure you are returning the product within the allowed time window.
- You will get emails keeping you abreast of your order delivery progress.
- After a certain amount of time, you will be asked to provide a product review. This is your chance to let the world know what you think.

Finding a product at amazon.com is also very easy. When you go there using your Internet browser, you can quickly just type the item you are looking for.

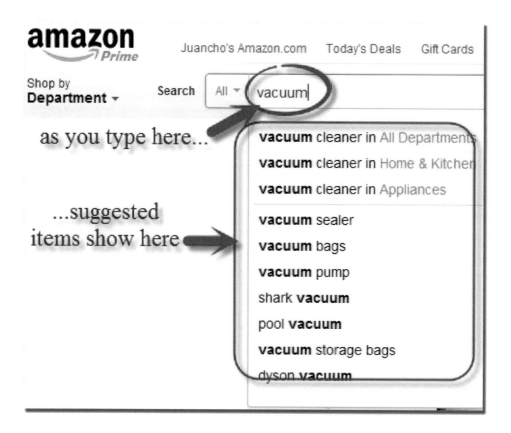

In this example, I'm looking for a vacuum. Here, you can see that the search starts making other suggestions about what you may be looking for. In this case I'm just looking for a vacuum appliance. I simply click the GO button, and I get results:

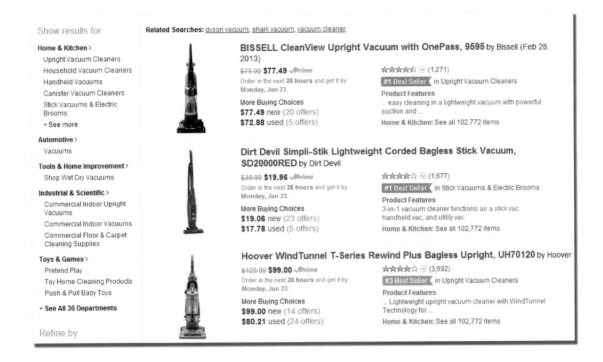

As you can see, you immediately get results, with the top list items having the best rating or being the best sellers. From here you can select a particular item, or you can narrow down your search using the filters on the left column. The filter options provided by amazon.com is extensive, to include review ratings and brand name.

When you select an item, you get details about the item like the following:

Roll over image to zoom in

Bissell CleanView with OnePass, 9595

by Bissell

★★★★☆ ▾ 1,271 customer reviews
| 239 answered questions

List Price: ~~$79.00~~
Price: **$77.49** ✓*Prime*
You Save: $1.51 (2%)

In Stock.
Ships from and sold by Amazon.com in easy-to-open packaging. Gift-wrap available.

Want it tomorrow, June 21? Order within 5 hrs 45 mins and choose **Saturday Delivery** at checkout. Details

Package Quantity: **1**

- Fast and easy cleaning in a lightweight vacuum with powerful suction and innovative brush design that cleans more on the initial pass.
- Innovative brush design rotates down into carpet to clean more on the initial pass.
- Cyclonic System for long-lasting, powerful suction.
- TurboBrush tool for stairs, furniture, upholstery, and more.
- Easy Empty dirt tank, Multi-Level Filtration, and washable foam tank filter.

You also get information about what other consumers have bought with this item, as well as which items other customers looking for vacuums have purchased.

Frequently Bought Together

Price for all three: **$92.11**

[🛒 Add all three to Cart]   [Add all three to Wish List]

Show availability and shipping details

☑ **This item:** BISSELL CleanView Upright Vacuum with OnePass, 9595 $77.49
☑ BISSELL Style 7/9/10 Replacement Belts, 2 pk, 32074 $4.63 [Add-on Item]
☑ Filter Pack (1 pre-motor & 1 post motor filter), 1008 $9.99

This is extremely helpful when you are shopping around. The **Frequently Bought Together** suggestion helps remind you of anything else you may need. The **Customers Who Bought This Item Also Bought** suggestions can help you find alternatives to the one you think you need. This is very helpful since the customer reviews and prices show in both sections.

These seemingly simple features make shopping on amazon.com a very delightful experience.

Internet Venues for Online Shopping

There are many venues or portals for online shopping. I already mentioned at least two of them. These are the most well-known for online shopping:

- Amazon.com
- Walmart.com
- eBay.com
- Google.com

These well-known venues or portals can generally be trusted to deliver what they sell or point you to an online store with appropriate customer ratings sufficient to keep vendors who wants to stay in business honest. In some cases, you can save on shipping.

At Amazon.com for example, if you are a Prime member, products that qualify can be delivered to you at no charge in a matter of two days.

At Walmart.com, you can have your item delivered to the nearest Walmart at no cost to you; just the cost of driving to that Walmart and the time to pick it up.

Determining Reliability of an Online Store

Sometimes the best deals show up online on some obscure e-commerce site. Fortunately most portals, like Google.com, eBay.com, and Amazon.com provide ratings for each online store.

The best way to assess a site's reputation and your potential experience with it is to read the comments from the lowest customer ratings. This will give you a sampling of the problems other customers have experienced with the site. In general you can tell what's reasonable and what isn't from peoples' complaints.

When you select a particular item to buy, Google Shopping will show you the different places where you can buy the item, and rates the seller at the advertised price. In this example, I was looking for a 15 inch laptop.

If you click **Compare prices from 3 stores**, you will see the ratings for the three stores selling this product.

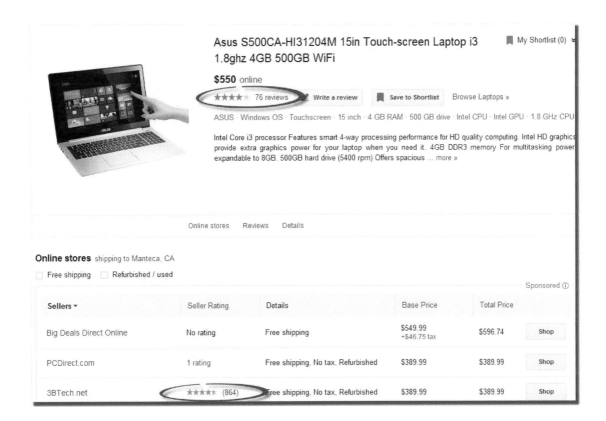

In addition to the seller rating, you will see product reviews to help you decide whether this is really the product you want. Anyway, in this example, only one seller has a viable rating, and the rating is greater than 4 from almost 900 consumers. The seller 3BTech.net looks like a reliable seller. Note that the other sellers aren't viable because they either don't have any rating or have very few ratings. You may be wondering where the threshold is for the number of ratings before an item is considered to have very few rating. Statistically, there is a way to figure this out using values for confidence level, confidence interval, and population size, but that would be overkill. Just read the reviews and use your gut instinct to figure out whether there is enough legitimate looking reviews there to support the actual rating. From my own experience, once they have over 10 reviews, you may have enough to make that determination.

I personally don't buy anything from any sellers with less than a 4 star rating. On the other hand, sellers with 4 or more stars can be relied upon to deliver the goods, in general. Of course there is no 100% guarantee in life, but highly rated sellers have a high likelihood of delivering.

Comparing Prices

Supposing that you've determined the most cost effective way to purchase that vacuum cleaner is by buying it online. Through Google Shopping (http://www.google.com/shopping), do a search for vacuum cleaner and sort by **Review score**. This way you get the most highly rated item to show up at the top.

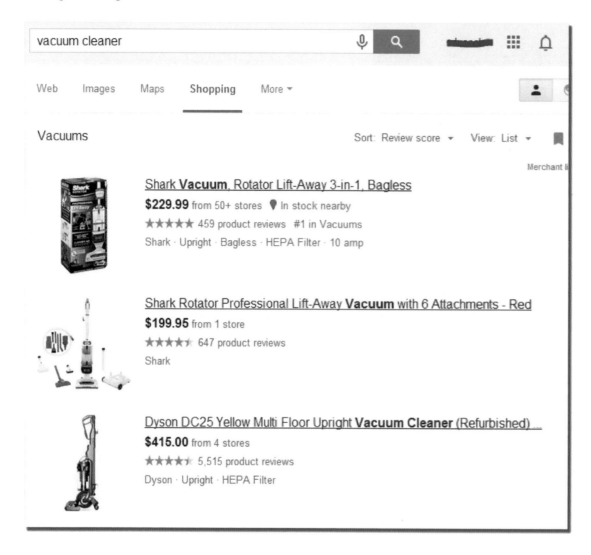

The Shark vacuum cleaner looks to be a good choice with a 5 star rating from 459 reviews. This isn't bad. The Dyson DC25 isn't bad either but for $415 for a refurbished unit, it seems way too expensive.

So if you click the first item, you will get more details about the product and where you can buy it. In this case, the price of $229.99 is through a company called "Shopko" which I've never heard of before; and it only has 2 seller reviews. I'm not sure I want to take a chance with that seller, but there are three other very well-known and established sellers that I can definitely trust. The lowest price is $244.99 from Sears. So instead of taking a chance at buying and saving around $15 from an unknown, I would choose $244.99 from Sears knowing that I can trust that seller to deliver.

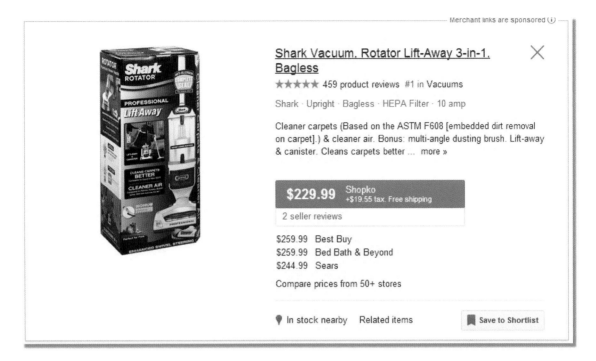

Thus, even though the lowest price is through Shopko, I know Sears is reliable for sure. Sears' total price is only about $15 above that of Shopko. I would purchase the vacuum through Sears knowing that I'm getting it from a reputable seller.

The moral of the story: "The least expensive priced item or seller isn't necessarily the best deal. You have to take into account buyer reviews of the product and the seller.

Role of Smart Phones

According to the Pew Research Center's Internet & American Life Project, 56% of US adults are smartphone owners.

 If you are part of that 56%, you can use your smartphone to help you get the best price while online or while shopping at a local store. All you need to do is install an APP on your smartphone that can scan the UPC (universal product code) bar code on a product and do a quick price comparison with online sources.

Google for example, has an app called Google Shopper (http://www.google.com/mobile/shopper). Install that on your phone and while shopping at a local store, you can quickly compare prices on items that interest you.

Here's how it would go.

1. You find an item you like.
2. On your phone, launch Google Shopper and scan the item's UPC bar code to get comparable item prices online.
3. The selection process is pretty much similar with what you do when you use your computer to make price comparisons.
4. If the item has no accessible bar code, just do a search in Google Shopper and you will get results just as you would using your computer's web browser.

This capability with the smartphone is really amazing. It is putting physical stores in a tough competitive situation. People are no longer confined to the boundaries of the physical stores, even when shopping within one.

Summary/Conclusion

Online Shopping is an essential skill today if you want to save money.

Sometimes you will find that it is still less expensive to buy from your local store. If not, you can use the local stores to get a feel of the physical aspects of the item you want to buy online.

Buying online requires that you know how to determine what the best price is in the market. You also need to know about some of the best Internet venues to do your online shopping.

And when faced with an online store you've never heard of, you can use your skill to determine the seller's reputation.

When you find that special item you've been looking for, you need to know how to compare the total price, which takes into account taxes and shipping charges.

Lastly, with the aid of a smartphone, you can be free from the limiting boundaries imposed by your local store, even when you are already there shopping.

You now know how to get the best deals online. Now go out and spend, and contribute to our ailing economy.

Online Selling

Why is online selling an essential Internet skill today? Well, if you could use the money, like most of us do, then you don't want to waste things you aren't using any more. Remember the old saying:

"Your junk is someone else's treasure."

Why not take advantage of this?

If you agree, then read on. You will learn about the different venues for selling your stuff, which allows you to go beyond your geographical limitations. This is all possible, thanks to the power of the Internet.

A Bit of History

"Garage sale" is what most people do when they are ready to sell stuff they no longer need. The process goes like this:

1. You realize you have more junk than you actually need, and decide it's time to clean house by doing a garage sale.
2. You put an ad in the local newspaper about your garage sale two weeks from now. It is to happen on a Saturday and a Sunday. No other days beyond this is practical since you work during the weekdays, and most people work on those days as well.
3. You start gathering up you junk in an area so you can at least be organized before the day of the garage sale.
4. The garage sale day arrives and you wake up before sunrise in order to set up just in front of your garage or house. Now you are set.

5. A few cars swing by; some come out and actually buy something, while most simply look around and leave.

6. At the end of the day, you have a smile on your face since you made a few dollars you didn't have before from junk you were going to throw out anyway.

That's how garage sales generally go.

Everything changed in 1995, when a company called eBay (http://goo.gl/pZcwCU) opened up. It was a simple online auction site for people who wanted to sell stuff. Back then, the Internet wasn't so mainstream as it is now, but things really picked up after 1996 when the Internet really became commercialized and ISPs (Internet Service Providers) made the Internet available to the masses. Remember dial up modems and the sound they made [http://goo.gl/k7of9x] (source: *Dialup Modem Noise, upto88.com*)? Remember how fast they went? Most were happy if they reached 44Kbps. Memories of the good ole days are certainly nice to think about, but surely, most wouldn't want to go back to it.

Fast forward to today.

Everyone has high-speed Internet access that go anywhere from 300Kbps and higher on the upload side, and 1 Mbps or higher on the download side. **NOTE***: If these numbers don't make sense to you, don't worry. Suffice it to say that Internet speeds today are orders of magnitude faster than in the late 1990s*. Anyway, almost half of the US population of cell phone users have smart phones that have Internet access and other capabilities.

With smart phones, you can pretty much connect to most Internet resources out there--including online shopping or selling sites.

Today, you have the ability to sell your junk anytime of the day, and any day of the week to almost anyone in the world you are willing to ship your stuff to. You are no longer confined to the local flea market or to setting up your own Sunday garage sale.

Today, you have access to the entire world when you want to sell your stuff. Isn't this awesome?

Prerequisites for Online Selling

If you want to have some chance at online selling, you'll need a few things set up as a bare minimum.

1. **Bank Account**. If you don't have one, make sure to get one. You'll need it to help make it easy to take in checks.

2. **Paypal Account**. You'll need this to give you the ability to handle credit cards or payment via Paypal.
3. **Post Office Box (or something equivalent)**. When people send in their payment or have to return things to you, you don't want to give them your home address. Instead, give them your PO Box address.
4. **Easy Access to Shipping**. Since you are dealing with physical things, you will need to ship things out. If you are close to a UPS, a FedEx, or a USPS, you are pretty much set. Some PO Box service providers also provides access to UPS, FedEx, and/or USPS.
5. **Online Selling Site Account**. You'll need at least one online selling site account (e.g. from eBay or Craigslist). You can't sell online without one of these, unless you setup your own eCommerce site, but that is beyond the scope of this article.

Venues for Online Selling

You cannot believe how many places allow you to sell. You are no longer confined to selling your garage sale junk; you can even sell things you make for a hobby, or stuff you purchased in bulk at an extremely low price!

I will categorize online selling sites as follows:

- **General**: sell pretty much anything here
- **Books**: sell old or new books here
- **Specialty**: you can sell specific things here
- **eCommerce**: If you want to setup your own online store

General

Below are online auction/selling sites for almost anything people will buy.

- eBay.com
- Craigslist.com
- amazon.com
- facebook.com
- offeritem.com
- us.ebid.net
- ubokia.com
- sell.com

Books

- alibris.com
- sellbackyourbook.com

- amazon.com

Specialty

- etsy.com - various merchandise
- gazelle.com - sell used electronics
- createspace.com - self publishing
- lulu.com - self publishing

eCommerce

- shopify.com
- wazala.com
- volusion.com
- bigcommerce.com
- webstore.amazon.com

Example: Selling on Craigslist.com

Let's go through an example using Craigslist.com as the selling venue. Here are the general steps to dealing with selling on Craigslist.com.

1. **Setup**. Setup an account on craigslist.com.
2. **Post Sale**. Post what you have on sale.
3. **Wait**. Wait for offers.
4. **Make the Sale**. Make the actual trade; your stuff for the buyer's dollars.

Setup

The first thing you need to do is setup a craigslist.com account; it's free. Follow these steps to create an account.

1. Using your Internet browser, go to http://craigslist.com and you will end up in the world map. You are supposed to identify your default location from this. You can scroll down and pick your town or a town close to your to set your default site, or you can simply use

the map to find your location. The rest of the steps below shows you how to use the map.

2. From this page, you need to identify your geographical location, or location that is closest to where you are. Keep clicking the plus sign until you find the most local craigslist.com site for your location.

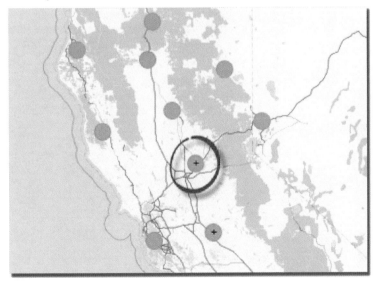

3. At some point, you will see circles with no PLUS sign in it. Those represent local craigslist.com sites.

In my case, I finally ended up at Stockton, CA. I clicked my location, and I end up here:

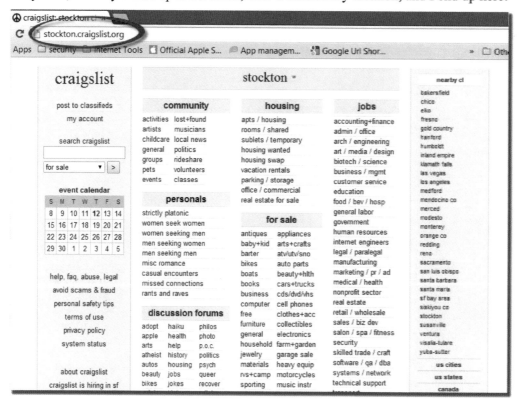

4. Next click the "my account" link.

It will take you to the login page. There click the "**Sign up for an account**" link.

<u>craigslist</u>: Account Log In

WARNING: scammers may try to steal your account by sending an **official-looking email** with a link to a **fake craigslist login page** that looks like this page, hoping you'll type in your username and password.

Look carefully at the web address
near the top of your browser to make sure you are on the real craigslist login page, https://accounts.craigslist.org

ory Bookmarks Tools Help

https://accounts.craigslist.org/

The safest way to login is go to the craigslist homepage directly by typing in the web address, and then clicking on the 'my account' link.

[more information]

Log in to your craigslist account

Email / Handle:

Password:

Log In forgot password?

Sign up for an account Why do I need an account?

You will end up here:

Enter your email address, then click create account. t shows this:

5. You are almost done. Now, all you have to do is check for an email from craigslist.com on the email address you registered. The following image shows how mine looks like. After I clicked the link activation link, it took me to craigslist.com so I can enter my selected password.

craigslist.org: New Craigslist Account itsensei@yahoo.com

craigslist - automated message, do not reply
To Me

Thank you for signing up for a craigslist account.
To log in to your account, please go to:
https://accounts.craigslist.org/pass?ui=232741905&ip=vWfaCTBl
You will be prompted to choose a password as soon as you log in.
If you experience any problems or have any questions, please reply to this message or email help@craigslist.org.
Thank you for using craigslist!

Reply, Reply All **or** Forward | More

Click this to activate the account

← → C 🔒 https://accounts.craigslist.org/pass?ui=232741905&ip=vWfaCTBl

🗀 Web Apps 🗀 security 🗀 Internet Tools 🗂 Official Apple S... 🗨 App managem... 🗂 God

Please enter a new password of your own choosing. Your new password must be 8 characters or more.

| Password: | |
| Re-type Password: | |

Submit Password and Log In

Questions? Please email help@craigslist.org.

Please enter a new password of your own choosing. Your new password must be 8 characters or more.

| Password: | ·········· |
| Re-type Password: | ·········· |

Submit Password and Log In

Craigslist comes back with this, if you met the minimum requirements for the password. At this point, you can click **Return to your account settings** or **Return to your account**.

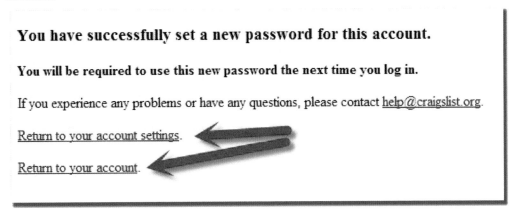

6. Regardless of which link you click, Craigslist will have you accept or decline their terms of use (TOU).

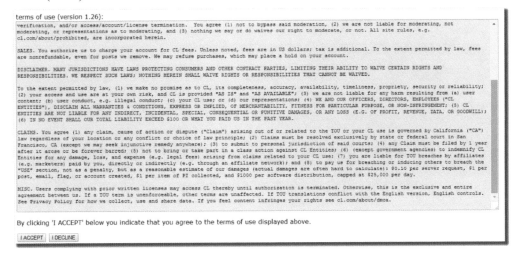

You have to click I ACCEPT if you wish to use craigslist, of course. Anyway, if you opted to Return to your account, you will end up here:

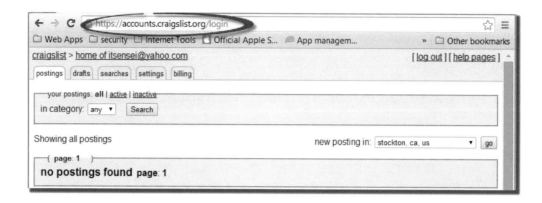

This just shows you the big picture, starting with any postings you may have. Since you just started, you won't have any.

7. Now click the settings tab to make sure the details of your account is set just the way you want it. The only field you'll want to update here is your default site (pointed to by the red arrow in the image).

If you are ever selling items that may not be practical to mail, or you just don't feel like dealing with checks or waiting for payment via mail, by specifying a default site, your sales can have a local presence--meaning that people in the surrounding areas will quickly see your posts.

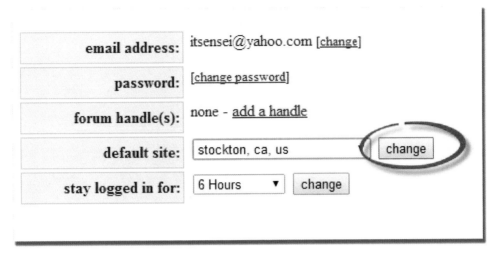

Once you've selected your location or default site, just click the **change** button (image above) and you will get the message "default site changed" as indicated by the red arrow (image below).

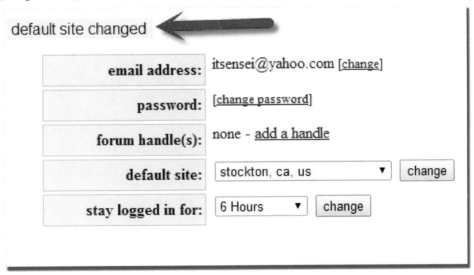

8. Your account is now fully setup. You can now post an ad to sell your stuff.

Post Sale

To post your first ad, just click the craigslist home page (where the red arrow points).

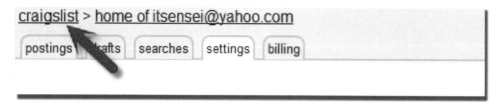

This will take you to your default craigslist site. In my case it is stockton.craigslist.org.

Now just click the link to **post to classifieds** and you are on your way to putting up your first ad.

Here are the steps to creating your first ad.

1. Once you click the **post to classifieds** link, you will end up at the "choose type" page. Since you are selling something, choose "for sale by owner."

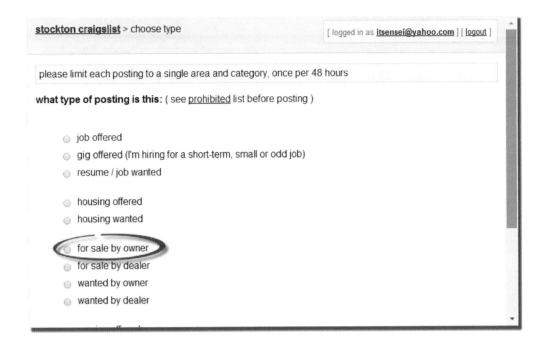

As you can see craigslist.com is more than a selling venue. You can actually post an ad for something you are looking for or even for a service you can offer, but those are topics of discussion for another time.

2. Next, craigslist takes you to choosing the category of sales you are posting. Pick a category and/or click **continue**.

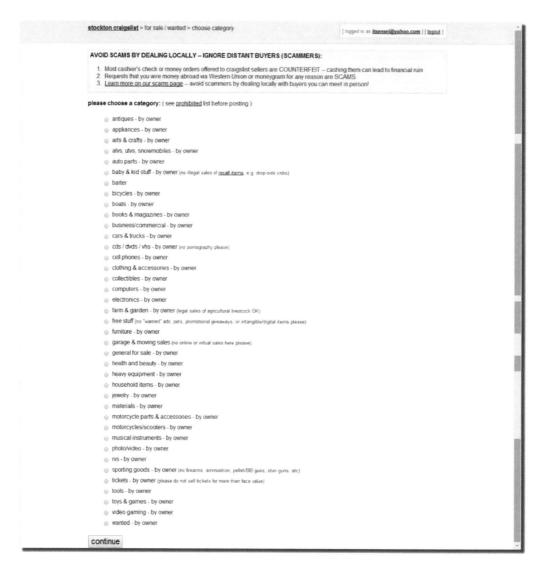

In most cases, picking a category will cause the page to jump to the **create posting page**. See following image.

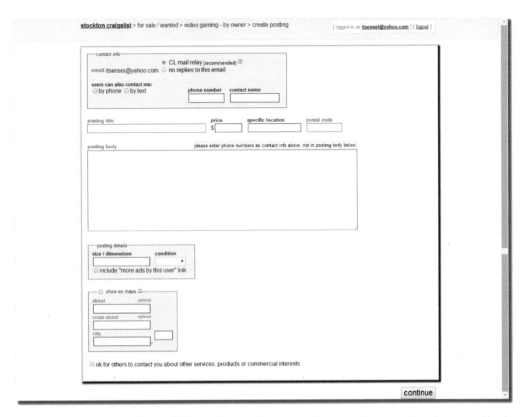

3. Complete the contact info section. If you wish, people to contact you by phone and/or by text. Check one or both, then enter the full phone number and a contact name.

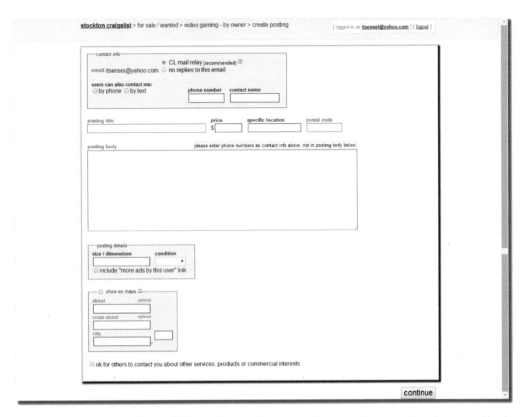

4. Next, complete the posting title and body section. First is the **posting title**. You need to come up with a catchy title so that your ad can stand out from the rest. Look at existing ads in your category to get some ideas.

Next, fill out the **price**. Do a bit of research here. As a matter of fact, just check for similar items in craigslist for like items and see how much they are selling. You don't want to make yours too high that no one would bother looking at your item. If you are desperate to sell fast, make sure to price your item lower than what the average is selling overall.

You can enter a **specific location** and **postal code** so that craigslist can figure out which other craigslist sites would be applicable to your ad.

Finally, enter the **posting body**. Provide as much detail as you can so that the potential buyer can truly understand what they are getting. The more information the better; this way the buyer will know exactly the condition of the item they are buying. This helps prevent future arguments about the sale.

posting title	price	specific location	postal code
	$		

posting body   please enter phone numbers as contact info above, not in posting body below.

5. The last section is the **posting details, show on map**, and **OK for others to contact you** options.

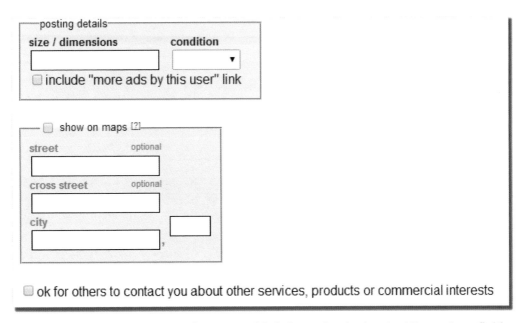

If your item has a size or dimension, enter this information in the **size/dimensions** field. Next pick a **condition**.

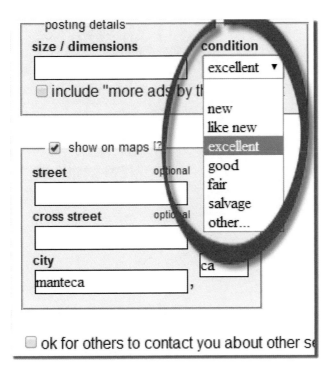

Condition is subjective, but your choices are: **new, like new, excellent, good, fair,**

salvage, and **other**. The newness of the item goes from highest to lowest, starting with "**new**" as the highest newness rating. "**Salvage**" then would be the lowest newness rating.

If you feel that you need to include **street** and **cross street**, you can include them, but they are optional. Do include city and state.

Lastly, leave the option for "ok for others to contact…" unchecked, unless you would like to receive sales/service solicitations.

6. Click the **CONTINUE** button on the bottom right side of the page.
7. If you specified a location, craigslist will take you to a page that will help further narrow down a location you wish to use when meeting people. Generally, the parking lot of a well-known store (like Walmart) is a good place to specify. When done, click **continue**.
8. At this point, you can post images of the item you are selling. Post as many pictures as you are allowed. The more pictures the better. It will give the buyer a better feel for what they are buying.

To post pictures, click the **Add Images** button. When done adding all your images or pictures, click the **done with images** button.

9. At this point, you have a draft of your ad. Review it until you are happy with what you see. When you are, click the **publish** button, and the whole world will see your posting.

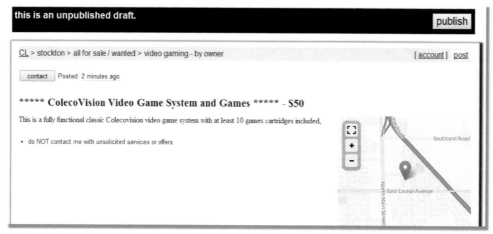

Wait

Now you wait.

You will be amazed at how fast a response you get. You'll get queries about your ad from email and your phone if you posted your number.

Eventually, you will rendezvous (or meet) with someone who is interested in purchasing your item. When you do, make sure to specify a location, like a major store parking.

For your own safety, make sure to meet where people can see you in the open, and/or have someone accompany you. Once you meet, the potential buyer will check out your item and most likely will make an offer that is lower than your posted price. That is to be expected since people are always looking to make a good deal, especially when they are the ones buying.

If you aren't happy with the offer, respectfully decline the offer. You could say something like "sorry, I can't really go lower than this price."

Make the Sale

At some point in time, someone will make the offer that meets your price. When you do and you are ready to collect the payment, make sure to take only cash. Remember, you are making a personal transaction, and if you take a check or money order, there is no way to figure out whether what you are receiving is legitimate or not. Most people that do direct person to person transaction on craigslist pay with cash.

Conclusion

You got junk? Now you don't have to settle for a garage sale. Sell stuff online 24 hours a day, and 7 days per week, to anyone who you can ship to and to anyone who will pay. If you have all the prerequisites, you are good to go.

Happy selling!

Final Thoughts on How to Use the Internet

With these seven key Internet tools and skills, you can navigate today's technologically charged world.

1. By knowing how to use your Internet browser, you have the basic foundation.
2. Through email you can establish you basic means of non-real-time electronic Internet communication.
3. By knowing how to use social networking tools, you can establish a useful network of online friend, relatives, and professionals.
4. Knowing how to text is crucial as well since this is a means of communication especially when phone service fails.
5. When you need to learn something, you need Internet research skills.
6. If you need something, online shopping skills can help you get it.
7. Lastly, when that something you have is no longer of use to you, you will need online selling skills to dispose of it and make money in the process.

All these tools and skills allow you to become a well-rounded Internet citizen with modern skills for success.

The Internet is an evolving system. Every few months, companies release newer and better products. Every year some new startup go online and provide new and interesting services.

Although the seven tools/skills discussed here will be useful for the years to come, other tools may become available to help improve your experience on the Internet.

Embrace the change, because only through this will you be able to conquer your fears of learning new things. Challenge yourself. You are capable of more things than you realize.

Resources

Note that the resources listed below are simply suggestions. As you browse at these possible further readings, you may find others that may interest you.

Some of the links are Amazon.com affiliate links which will take you to Amazon.com. The books have at least a review rating of 4 stars or higher.

Internet Browsers
- Book: Web Geek's Guide to Google Chrome (http://amzn.to/1neTOzo) by Jerri Ledford and Yvette Davis
- Free online resources
  - Chrome Help (https://support.google.com/chrome/) by Google Support
  - Getting Started with Internet Explorer 11 (http://goo.gl/AcGXyl) by Microsoft Support
  - Getting Started with Firefox (http://goo.gl/fbXQRD) by Mozilla Support

Email
- Book: Google gmail (http://amzn.to/1llG6MJ) by Steve Schwartz
- Free online resources
  - Yahoo Mail (https://overview.mail.yahoo.com/) by Yahoo.com
  - Google's Gmail (https://support.google.com/mail/) by Google Support

Social Networking
- Books:
  - Facebook for Dummies (http://amzn.to/1hSybWv) by Carolyn Abram
  - Teach Yourself VISUALLY Facebook (http://amzn.to/1pKea3Y) by Ben Harvell
  - What the Plus!: Google+ for the Rest of Us (http://amzn.to/1nGhZtT) by Guy Kawasaki
  - The Twitter Book (http://amzn.to/1n1zscQ) by Tim O'Reilly
- Free Online training: The Beginner's Guide to Facebook (http://goo.gl/8EQniS) by Grovo.com
- Free online resource: Getting Started with Google+ (http://goo.gl/RraJe5) by Google.com

TEXTing
- Book: Text Messaging Survival Guide (http://amzn.to/1llGFGn) by Evie Shoeman

- Free Android App: textPlus Free text + calls from Android phones, tablets, and Kindle Fire by textPlus, Inc. (http://amzn.to/1lqp2zg)

Internet Research
- Book: Google Power Search (http://amzn.to/1kU9DMv) by Stephan Spencer
- Free online resources
  - Google Advanced Search (http://goo.gl/yYcPuM) by Google.com
  - How to Search on Google (http://goo.gl/zCTdJ0) by Google.com
  - Basic Search Help (http://goo.gl/RLMUf4), by support.google.com
  - Operators and More Search Help (http://goo.gl/bCO0i3), by support.google.com
  - Search Results Options and Tools (http://goo.gl/l8bS0s), by support.google.com

Online Shopping
- Free Android App: Saviry - Deals, Freebies, Sales - best online shopping (http://amzn.to/1ve17us) by Lanuta. This is an Android phone or tablet app. There may be a corresponding one for the iPad or iPhone.
- Free online resource: How to get Reduced Prices and Save Money when Shopping on Amazon (http://goo.gl/WbggWe) by Adam Dachis at lifehacker.com

Online Selling
- Book: From Trash to Cash: Sell Your Junk on eBay, Craigslist and Gumtree with this proven guide (http://amzn.to/1ljzLLK) by Mr. Alex McClafferty
- Free online resource: Getting Started Selling on eBay (http://goo.gl/zJY6h7) by eBay.com
- Online garage sales
  - www.garagesales.com
  - www.garagesale.com
  - www.yardsale123.com
  - www.theonlineyardsale.com

Index

About the Author

Juancho Forlanda is a full time Information Technology (IT) manager at a major school district in the Central Valley, in California. At night he is a martial arts instructor (along with his wife and two daughters), helping kids and adults alike become better people through the character and success building exercises ingrained in the classes.

When he's not working, he is spending time with his family at home; and when he's not doing this, he is working on his hobbies and other activities like running, writing, and computing.

Juancho Forlanda is an avid writer and has written many articles on various topics online through sites like hubpages.com (at http://forlanda.hubpages.com/), InsideTechnology360.com (Man Evolves Technology to Fit His Needs— http://goo.gl/3sq9jt) and brighthub.com (http://goo.gl/FFiyFG will list his various technical articles at brighthub.com). He also maintains his martial arts web site and his personal site at www.koryoftc.com and www.forlanda.net, respectively, where he writes about topics related to success concepts, running, and technology.

His educational credentials include a Bachelor of Science degree in Electrical Engineering with focus on digital electronics, and a Master of Science degree in Computer Systems with emphasis on computer networks and database systems.

If you wish to contact him about this book or other related subject matter, you can reach him directly via his email at forlanda@gmail.com.

34241074R00074

Made in the USA
Charleston, SC
01 October 2014